HAMLYN

Cage and Aviary
Birds

CONTENTS:

INTRODUCTION

When we use the term cage birds we usually have the exotic species of the tropics and subtropics in mind. A great number breed well in captivity and many species such as the Budgerigar, Cockatiel, lovebirds, Zebra Finch and others live in captivity for several generations. The keeping of such exotic species in no way disrupts their natural population, but the same is not true of European and North American birds whose numbers, especially in recent years, have been markedly declining due to man's various interventions. Many of these are migratory birds that suffer great losses every year and it is therefore only right that most of them are protected and that it is prohibited to catch them. Furthermore, with the exception of a very few species, they do not nest in cages. Bird fanciers, especially beginners, would thus do well to obtain a species that is already commonly reared in captivity and in this way further the protection of birds and nature in general.

WHERE AND HOW TO OBTAIN BIRDS

Every new aviculturist wants to have birds that are healthy, eat well and perhaps even multiply, and for this reason it is best to start by purchasing birds directly from an experienced bird-keeper. If one does not know of any, one can turn for advice to an avicultural society which can be found in most large cities. Buying a bird directly from a breeder is usually somewhat more expensive than purchasing an imported specimen oneself, but it has certain advantages. First of all the bird has been born in captivity in the conditions of the local environment and is therefore well acclimatized. One can ascertain its exact age, that it comes from healthy stock, and also the kind of food it eats. Commonly reared birds can also be obtained in a pet shop, though in this case their parentage and exact age are generally not known. The purchase of birds from foreign aviculturists or dealers is another possibility, and although restrictions are laid on the export from and import of birds into other countries (and it would be wise to investigate these if considering exporting birds from them), at the present time in the United Kingdom there are no restrictions on the importing of the cage birds described in this book. The Home Office restricts the import of the Common Quail, Lapwing, and any ducks or geese at certain times of the year. Birds of prey and owls also carry some restrictions and a licence must be issued by the Home Office to import these. The Ministry of Agriculture also places some restrictions on importing poultry and pheasants. These restrictions are all covered in The Poultry and Hatching Eggs Order, the Protection of Birds Act 1954 and the Wild Birds Importation Order 1970.

PRINCIPLES OF BIRD-KEEPING

Whoever decides to become an aviculturist starts out by buying birds in pairs whenever possible, so that they will nest and rear young. First of all the beginner will need a cage, preferably a large one, or a smaller aviary, as birds nest more readily if they have ample space. Those who are able to place the aviary in a garden will provide their birds with a natural environment, and warm-loving species with ample sun in summer. Even small birds should be given the greatest possible amount of space to allow ample room for flying. One of the most important conditions for successful bird-keeping is fresh air, but care must be taken to avoid draughts and to provide sufficient light. Only part of and not the whole cage should be exposed to direct sunlight for most birds also need shade. Two other important factors are adequate moisture, attained by means of a mist-spraying apparatus, and of course cleanliness, which is a must.

A good type of cage is one with only the front side open but covered with wire netting, for the birds are thus provided with greater protection and are therefore less easily frightened. All-wire cages, open on all four sides, are well suited for the peaceable and tamer birds, but even these should be so placed as to have the rear side protected, e. g. against a wall. In winter the cage should not be placed close to a window because of the cold air outside, but in warm, summer weather the birds will benefit if the cage, partially shaded, is placed in the window, though not in really hot sun. Fresh branches should be kept in the cage or aviary and replaced by new ones every now and then to help keep the cage clean. They are also welcomed by many species such as parrots, which enjoy nibbling at the bark.

Food or vessels containing food should never be placed directly beneath a branch or perch on which the birds often rest as they will become soiled by droppings. The best place is on the outside of the cage so that the food can easily be reached by the birds but yet remains clean. It is also important to supply the cage with a shallow bath big enough for the birds to bathe in comfortably — many do so frequently and enjoy it. The floor of the cage should be covered with clean, washed sand and if a sheet of paper is used instead, then sand should be supplied in a shallow vessel, for it is a necessary part of a bird's diet, helping to grind the food in the stomach.

Keeping foreign birds as well as the care of more common species requires knowledge of each one's habits and the food it eats in the wild. Only thus can one provide the birds with conditions at least approximating those of their natural habitat. This is especially important in the case of newly imported and freshly captured birds, some of which refuse substitute food. They should be given food as similar as possible to that which they subsist on in the wild state and then gradually taught to eat food that is readily available. Should a newly acquired bird not feed from the floor of the cage or aviary at first, it is recommended that the food and even the water vessel be placed higher up for a few days. Then, when the birds have become acclimatized, the vessels can be placed on the floor.

HOW TO CARE FOR BIRDS–GENERAL MANAGEMENT

On acquiring a new bird, especially one of the smaller species, which is more active and capable of rapid flight, one should first put it carefully in a cage, even though an aviary may be available. Being unused to a larger space such birds may crash into the wire mesh and injure themselves or even die if they try to fly. Later, when ready to be transferred to a roomier aviary, they should be placed in it inside the cage, with the door open so that each bird can fly out by itself into its new and larger surroundings. Many bird-keepers do let their pets fly freely about the room. However, even in this instance the bird must first become accustomed to the cage, which it soon comes to regard as its home, and only then should it be let out, returning to the cage of its own accord. The first time it is released it should be carefully watched in case it flies into the closed windows. Becoming accustomed to flying about outside the cage, therefore, must also be a gradual process and to start with it is recommended that the curtains are drawn so that the bird will see the obstacle and avoid it. Later it will learn to avoid even an uncovered window. Another point to remember is that birds do not tolerate smoke — it may even make them ill — and therefore there should be no smoking in the room where they are kept.

It is often necessary to catch the bird, when transferring it to different quarters, or disinfecting the cage, for example. In the case of a small bird this is best done without gloves for bare hands have greater sensitivity. Making a hollow in the palm of the hand, the bird should be held lightly between the thumb and fingers so that it cannot flap its wings or thrash about. It should be remembered that for many a bird being caught in the hand can be quite frightening. For stronger birds which have a sharp bite one can put on a light glove. Parrots cause the greatest difficulty, especially the larger birds which can easily nip through a light glove. In such cases, e. g. an Amazon parrot, macaw or parakeet, a fine cloth can be thrown over the bird's head and body so that it cannot see, and it should then be grasped on either side of the head near the beak so that it cannot bite. Toucans are better grasped from above, holding the upper and lower beak together.

Birds in captivity rarely have as much exercise as in the wild, due to the limitations of space, and also because they do not need to spend hours searching for food. Since they are deprived of the natural opportunities for normal wear of their beaks and claws, these often become overgrown and the birds are unable to feed properly or perch comfortably. In such cases it is necessary to trim the claws and clip or file the beak. To do this the bird should be grasped in the left hand and the claws cut with nail clippers, for they can split if normal scissors are used. The claw should not be cut too close, otherwise the vein running down the middle can be damaged and can bleed. This sometimes happens when the bird itself breaks its nail. In this case, the claw should be bandaged for a time or else a preparation applied that will stop the bleeding. Even if it bleeds profusely it is not dangerous, but should be treated. Naturally it is best to try and prevent such a mishap and therefore the claws should be trimmed with great care. If the bird-keeper is inexperienced it is better to get it done by a vet. As for the beak, it should first be cut with nail scissors to its original shape and then trimmed carefully with a fine nail file, all the while holding the bird by the sides of the head. The task really requires two persons, so that the one doing the cutting has both hands free. Here, too, the inexperienced beginner would do better to have it done by a specialist.

Sometimes a male which has been caged for a long time may start pursuing the female without let-up, with the result that she becomes unable to eat. In this case the male must be caught and a few of its primary feathers on one wing trimmed, thus making it more difficult for him to move about the cage and allowing the female to escape with ease. A better method is to pluck the primary feathers carefully, for once cut new ones will not grow in until the moulting period, whereas in the first instance they do so immediately. Even so the interval is long enough for the cock to calm down. If a bird breaks one of its long feathers, e. g. in the tail or wing, and is consequently hampered in its movements, the feather should be plucked out whole and not cut. However they must be mature feathers; newly growing ones should never be pulled out as this causes profuse bleeding.

If they are to be transported some distance, birds are carried or shipped in boxes made of wood, as a rule. These vary in size and sometimes have small openings or even one whole side made of wire mesh. This is particularly important for larger birds in order that they have sufficient air on the journey. Inside the box should be a perch and for longer journeys it should also be supplied with a firmly anchored food and water vessel. It is wise to put a piece of sponge, peat or moss in the dish so that the water does not get splashed during transport. In the case of seed-eaters, seeds can be strewn on the floor of the box; for parrots and other fruit-eaters some juicy fruit should be added which contains a lot of water. The top of the box should be covered with a layer of soft rubber so that the bird does not injure its head; in the case of small birds a piece of cloth will do. Parrots must have firm boxes, preferably made of hard wood which cannot be split with their strong beaks, and cloth should not be stretched under the top as they might easily tear it and get entangled in the shreds.

The travelling box must not be too large but should be big enough to give the bird a certain amount of freedom and room to feed in comfort. If the box is equipped with wire netting somewhere this should be covered with a translucent fabric, so that the birds have sufficient light but are unable to see out and therefore remain undisturbed by the movement and changing environment on the journey.

CAGES AND AVIARIES

Beginners will do best to purchase a ready-made, all-wire cage. The floor is a metal tray which can be slid out for easy cleaning and change of sand or paper. Around the cage is a protective band of glass several centimetres high that prevents food remnants from falling or being thrown out of the cage. Many seeds are in fact oily and can make grease spots on the floor or carpet. On one side of the cage there is usually a glass bath attached to the outside with an opening which can be closed. The nest, or nesting box can likewise be hung on the outside and entered through an opening in the side of the cage. This arrangement provides the birds with the greatest possible amount of space. The food and water vessels are usually located at the sides in the lower part of the cage and they, too, can be slid in and out. The cage may be placed in any spot, but always so that direct sunlight falls on it from the side at some time during the day.

Two other kinds of cage are the semi-box and box type with three sides, or three sides and the top of plywood. In these, the birds have greater quiet and the boxes can be stacked or placed side by side without the birds disturbing one another, as they cannot see into the other cages. The inside of the box is painted white to provide as much light as possible.

Cages can look very attractive hanging on the wall adjoining the window wall. They can be quite long so that the birds have plenty of room. The food vessels and nesting boxes are generally hung at the sides and with tasteful arrangement of the rest of the furniture such cages can become an attractive element of the interior decor.

Special cages, especially bigger ones, are not available in the shops as a rule and the bird-keeper must have such a cage made to order according to his design, or else make it himself. The cages can be all wire, of wire netting stretched over a wooden framework or of wires passed through holes drilled in wooden laths. In the case of a metal framework the wires are soldered. But because the cage has to be disinfected occasionally, usually with a mixture of water and various disinfecting agents which destroy wood, preference should be given to an all-wire cage. Spraying with water to provide the birds with adequate moisture also has an unwelcome effect on wood. For this reason wooden constructions should be given a coat of paint, which is also recommended for the wire and metal parts so that they do not rust. The size of the cage naturally depends on the size of the birds and the available space.

Plants should not be put in smaller cages but are strongly recommended in larger, roomier ones, especially if their occupants are birds that nest in thickets in the wild, in which case one can put a clump of reeds, dried and cut down to size in a rear corner. The individual stems can be made to stand firm by inserting them in a lump of clay covered with a sprinkling of sand and moss. A thickly covered branch or evergreen plant in a flowerpot is excellent for birds whose natural habitat is the undergrowth, but this is not recommended for birds that bite and destroy vegetation, for example many species of parrots. Greenery in the cage has the added advantage that it must be watered regularly, thus ensuring the requisite level of humidity inside the cage. Another type of cage is the cupboard type, consisting of separate cages, each with its own door and pull-out floor, arranged either side by side or on top of one another. This is not very practical, however, for the food and water vessels must be placed inside and is much better suited for the large-scale housing of canaries.

The perch is an important item in the cage and must be scrubbed and cleaned thoroughly at least once a week. The reason for this is that the birds use the perch to sharpen their beaks on, and it becomes soiled not only by their excreta and possibly the eggs of parasites, but also by food remnants, and the resulting decaying processes may easily infect the bird and cause various diseases. Best of all, therefore, are removable perches fixed between two opposite wires. Submitting them to a hot steam bath is an excellent means of destroying any disease germs. Many bird-keepers prefer natural perches, e.g. a twiggy branch of hazel or poplar, etc., for not only does it provide a natural resilient surface but furthermore requires no cleaning, being burnt and then replaced by a new branch, thus completely destroying all sources of infection.

Those who have ample space can build an indoor aviary. A smaller one is not much different from a large cage except that it cannot be moved and is generally built permanently in a light spot which has partial sunlight. It is important that such an aviary gets direct light from a window. An aviary can be easily constructed by anyone who is handy with tools, for it is really nothing more than a wooden or metal framework covered with strong wire netting, according to the type of bird it is to hold. On one side is a door for entry, and the back and one side can be formed by the corner walls of the room, which should have a washable surface or else one from which dirt can easily be removed. The aviary should contain a piece of tree trunk, a stout branch with smaller branches, or natural perches fastened to the wall. The trunk and perches should be washed from time to time with hot water to which a little soda has been added, and then rinsed. The tree trunk should be replaced by a new one once a year when the aviary is given a thorough cleaning. A strong pear, apple or lime tree branch will also serve the purpose quite well.

The floor of the aviary may be of plastic or linoleum, i.e. any material that is impervious to moisture. This is covered with a layer of sand which should be raked daily to remove food remnants and droppings and replenished as required. More plants can be put in the aviary than in a cage, but not in the case of birds that would destroy them. Food vessels should be placed on the floor, but not under the branches and best of all close to the door. The same goes for the bath. The size of the bath depends on the size of the birds. Photo-developing trays of varying dimensions serve the purpose very well. Flat stones should be placed inside to aid birds in getting out of the water, for some become thoroughly soaked when bathing. The amount of water in the bath again depends on the type of bird. For small birds it should be less than 2.5 cm (1 in) deep, for a bird that stands in water it should reach to the tarsus. Even better is a bath with a gradually sloping bottom so that the bird can choose the depth it wants, but a few flat stones should also be included. The bath should be placed on a thicker layer of sand or sawdust for the birds are apt to do quite a bit of splashing.

Nesting boxes should be hung on the wall. Plants for nesting birds are best placed in the rear corner of the aviary. The whole aviary should be lightly sprayed with tepid water from time to time and it does not hurt the birds if they get sprayed too. The greenery may also be put in flowerpots attached to the wall and masked with bark.

A light attic room or glass porch or entrance hall are likewise good places for an indoor aviary, but it must be possible to heat them in winter.

Some bird-keepers attach a smaller aviary or larger cage to the outside of a window linked with the indoor aviary so that the birds may go out in summer whenever they like. Such aviaries are excellent in cities where the bird-keeper does not have sufficient space for an outdoor aviary.

The most important thing to remember is not to put too many birds even in a larger aviary. Most species avidly defend their territory during the nesting season and this could result in unnecessary battles and losses. Moreover, some species cannot be housed together at all, and even when they do tolerate other kinds, it is necessary to be careful in the choice of new companions introduced to the cage. This, of course, should never be done during the nesting period. New birds should be put in the aviary in the morning and the reaction of the other occupants to their presence watched throughout the day, so as to forestall any possible disaster by removing the new members in time. The best method is to put all the birds one plans to have there into the aviary at the same time so that there is no problem of previously established territories, since the environment is new to all.

A special type of aviary is one comprising a whole separate room. This, of course, is only possible for the bird-keeper who lives in a house or a large flat. Such an aviary has no wire netting except on the windows during the summer months. The inside can be fitted out according to the bird-keeper's individual tastes, the same as in a smaller aviary. One advantage, however, is that one has more leeway in the placing of the plants and can make a larger nesting ground, for example using reeds, etc. Tree trunks with branches should be placed some distance from the walls so as not to soil the latter. Nesting boxes should be hung on large boards attached to the wall, as the birds often perch on the tops of the boxes, thereby also soiling the walls. A branch is usually affixed beside the entrance hole to the nesting box, allowing the nesting pair to perch there. The heater in such an aviary should be entirely covered with wire netting of thicker mesh, and a similar protective covering should be placed on radiators and pipes in the case of a central heating system. The reaction of the bird's organism to repeated contact with heat is similar to that caused by freezing; it may even lose one or more entire toes after several weeks. The door to the room should be covered by reeds or some other hanging foliage or it may be furnished with a wire-netting, double-door arrangement. Despite its size even such an aviary requires careful selection of its occupants, i. e. species that will tolerate each other. One of the disadvantages of this larger type of aviary is the difficulty of catching an ill or injured bird. Generally this is done with the aid of a catch-cage, for otherwise the bird is needlessly weakened by the length of time it eludes its captor.

Those who are lucky enough to have a garden will doubtless erect an outdoor, summer aviary in which some species can be kept right through the winter. The part of this book dealing with the various species states whether the bird can survive the winter outside in its respective description. Less hardy birds are transferred to the outdoor aviary in spring, April or early May depending on the weather, and are returned to their heated quarters in the autumn, late September or October.

An outdoor aviary should be rectangular, one quarter to one third roofed, and the back wall and a quarter to one third of the side walls solid, generally of wooden planks. Smaller aviaries up to 3 m (9½ ft) in length should be half-roofed, so that the birds have sufficient protection from the rain as well as shelter for the night and against predators. The height should be 1.8—2 m (5—6 ft), the length from 3—6 m (9—12 ft) or even 10 m (32 ft), depending on the bird-keeper. In larger aviaries it is possible to keep smaller species of pheasant along with the various cage birds. The aviary should be at least 1.5 m (4½ ft) long and ideally about 2.5 m (7½ ft) wide, according to the possibilities afforded by individual gardens.

Outdoor aviaries may also be constructed with the rear part resembling a house through whose windows the birds enter the aviary proper. The shelter provides the birds with a place to nest and protection against bad weather and predators. Hardy birds can easily be kept in such an aviary without a source of heat as long as they have shelter throughout the winter.

The ground under outdoor aviaries may be sown with grass or covered with turf and planted with a variety of suitable bushes and small trees such as loniceras or various conifers like pine, spruce, juniper, etc., in whose thick branches many birds like to build their nests. It is also possible to plant reeds or clumps of sedge and arrange the tree trunks in various ways — in fact anything is in order which pleases the eye and is suitable for the particular birds.

In an outdoor aviary it is possible to build a shallow pool of concrete containing several flat stones and pebbles to help the birds get out. The floor of the pool should be sloping and undulating and it should be encircled with a thicker layer of sand.

The door of the aviary should be located at the rear of the side wall and it is recommended that a double-door arrangement of wire netting be constructed in front of it to prevent the birds flying out when one enters. When erecting the aviary it is a good idea to include a removable frame in the wall which allows the bird-keeper to enter with a wheelbarrow to remove old soil and bring in new soil, sand, turf, stones, tree trunks, etc. This is done in the spring or autumn and when the aviary is unoccupied.

One of the dangers of the outdoor aviary is that the birds are exposed to attacks by vermin, mainly Weasels, Polecats, martens, as well as Brown Rats, domesticated cats and owls. The first four animals can squeeze through an unbelievably small opening as well as burrow underneath the soil, and for this reason it is important that the aviary be constructed with a concrete foundation wall, extending into the soil to a depth of at least 80 cm (32 in). The wire netting should fit snugly against this foundation. The foundation wall should be topped with a 30—50 cm (12—20 in) high band of wood around the entire circumference to keep mice, rats and martens which run about outside the enclosure from frightening the birds. Excellent protection is also provided by a double layer of wire netting.

Aviaries with a shelter at the back make good protection against such unwelcome visitors, which frighten the sleeping birds by climbing up the wire netting, causing them to fly up and dash against it in the dark, whereupon the predator can seize them by the foot and perhaps even tear it off; the wounded bird then bleeds to death. For this reason it is most important that the birds have at least partial shelter, and the bird-keeper who erects even a simple aviary should at least cover the back and one third of each side, say, with straw matting.

In smaller aviaries it is possible to build the foundation of bricks, but these must fit tightly, for many vermin are capable of scratching their way even through mortar. Old or cracked wire glass can also be put down into the earth. Nevertheless, it is necessary to place traps near the aviary and rid the surroundings of as much vermin as possible.

FOOD AND FEEDING

Suitable and, where possible, natural foods are one of the most important factors in bird-keeping. Every bird-keeper should be acquainted with at least the basic natural diet of his various caged birds. In the wild, each bird has an unlimited selection — every month of the year provides a different kind of food and the bird-keeper should do the same by giving the birds the food that is in season as a supplement to their daily, staple diet.

From the aviculturist's viewpoint, caged birds are divided into two main groups — seed-eaters and insectivores. The former feed primarily on seeds, though they also eat insects and similar live foods, especially when feeding their young. Insectivores eat mainly insects or feed on soft fruits, juices and the like.

Food is therefore divided into several basic groups:

I SEEDS AND GRAINS

This food is usually kept in stock in greater quantities. It may be purchased from a special shop or else grown or collected by the aviculturist himself. Seeds should be absolutely clean, without any dust, and must not be stored in a damp place where they might easily get mouldy. They must not be rancid and this applies especially to oil seeds. Food infested by the Storehouse Mite *(Acarus siro)* is likewise harmful. Seeds are generally given to the birds in the form of seed mixtures, so that they can select what they want themselves. The stock of seeds should always be in adequate proportion to the number of captive birds and should be replenished regularly. The basic seeds are as follows:

1. Sunflower seed. These can either be purchased or gathered from plants growing in the garden or cultivated in a small field. One's own harvest has the advantage of being fresh and of good quality, but one must not forget to let the sunflowers attain full ripeness. Sunflower seeds can be fed to all species of seed-eaters except smaller birds which find them too large.

2. Canary seed. This is a great favourite with birds. It is suitable for all small species of seed-eaters. Canary seed is the seed of a Canary Islands grass but in recent years it has also been grown in Europe.

3. Millet. Of the several kinds of millet the most common is the white (pale yellow) variety. It is one of the most widely used foods for all finches and small parrots.

4. Hemp seed. This is given only in small quantities and primarily in winter. Larger quantities might cause the birds to get fat, for hemp seed is very oily. It is given chiefly to birds that are in a weakened condition and those that winter in a colder room or outdoors. For smaller birds it is served crushed, e. g. by pressing with a roller over a piece of paper, so that the meat is more easily extracted.

5. Niger seed. This is very good as food but should be given in small quantities. It is a glossy black seed slightly resembling cummin seed, and is imported chiefly from Africa.

6. Flax seed. Some species of birds eat this while others do not In small quantities it provides a good variation to the diet.

7. Rape seed. This is very good food for Fringillidae (finch-type birds), especially canaries, and contains many necessary nutrients. Best of all is the variety which has a slightly sweet taste, is small and coloured dark red to black. Rape seed is usually given separately and not mixed with other seeds.

8. Poppyseed. This is a good food supplement, but only in small quantities, and best of all fed together with an egg mixture.

9. Oats. Hulled or slightly crushed, this is a very good food for it contains proteins and little fat and is easily digested. It must be absolutely clean and is added to mixtures.

10. Lettuce seed. This is given in small quantities to smaller species of birds as a welcome change in diet.

11. Buckwheat. A good variation of the diet, given in small quantities.

12. Rice. This is only suitable for certain species of birds. It should be served unhulled or slightly boiled.

13. Wheat. This can be given to larger seed-eaters and parrots in small quantities.

14. *Maize*. This is suitable only for large species of parrots either in small quantities or whole unripe ears. Such ears can be given to all parrots.

15. *Radish seed*. In small amounts it supplies added variety to the diet.

16. *Seeds of various grasses and plants* the bird-keeper can gather himself. Whole sprays may be put in the cage, even ones that are not fully ripe.

17. *Thistle seeds*. These provide a suitable supplement to the diet.

18. *Seeds from cones* of various trees such as pine, spruce, etc. Some birds may even be given ripe Alder cones.

All the above seeds when given in small quantities are a suitable food and provide welcome change in the diet.

Birds find ears of grain inviting and almost all birds like them in this form. The ones most commonly given are the ears of millet, oats, maize, plantain, etc., always in the unripe state. Seeds may be soaked or allowed to germinate before being given to the birds. Germinating seeds are a suitable food for all seed-eaters.

Certain bird-keepers make up various seed mixtures containing the greatest possible amount of necessary nutrients. The ideal mixture for finch-type birds should contain canary seed, white millet, Indian millet and niger seed. For canaries: rape seed, canary seed, niger seed, hemp seed, hulled oats, poppyseed, radish seed and lettuce seed. For Budgerigars: millet, canary seed, hulled oats, etc.

II GREEN FOOD

Green food is an important supplement to the diet of almost all cage birds, for in their natural habitat birds nibble the green parts of plants, shoots, buds, grass and the like.

Lettuce is the most common green food, though not the most suitable as it causes diarrhoea in many birds. For this reason it should be given in small quantities and unsprayed by insecticides. Other suitable green foods are spinach, dandelion, plantain, milfoil, chickweed, green rape stalks, Lucerne and fine grass. When giving spinach it is also necessary to supply a greater quantity of eggshells, Cuttlefish bones and other mineral substances. In winter, the bird-keeper can sow wheat, which quickly germinates in a warm environment, in an indoor box in a warm and light room and thus have green food with which to feed his charges at any time during the winter months. The same can be done with maize. Another good, green food supplement is Spiderwort, which has a rapid growth. In summer, duckweed can be gathered from the surface of ponds and pools, where it grows in abundance.

Dried green food is likewise a good supplement to the winter diet. The commonest is Lucerne meal or dried Lucerne crumbs, i. e. the crushed leaves, and even dried nettles. Dried green food is usually added to 'soft' mixtures.

The twigs of fruit trees, willows, etc. (even with the blossoms) are likewise considered good green food.

III FRUITS

Many species of birds feed on fruits in their natural habitat, and these should therefore also be fed to them in captivity. Some birds are only fruit-eaters. Fruits recommended even for small seed-eaters are apples, pears, cherries and tropical fruits such as oranges and bananas. A good dietary supplement for some birds are strawberries, raspberries and blueberries. Even dried Rowan berries can be given on occasion, especially during the winter months. At this time, when there is a lack of fresh fruit, these may be supplied in stewed form diluted with water.

Honey is another food which can be added to the artifical 'nectars' fed to certain birds. It is a very good supplement.

IV CARROTS

This is listed separately because it is a basic item in the diet of almost all cage birds. It is given whole to larger parrots, boiled and diced to toucans, but for most birds it is best grated raw and added to the egg mixture.

V ANIMAL FOOD

This is very important not only for insectivorous birds but also for seed-eaters. First on the list is egg, served as a rule in egg mixtures. It should be hardboiled and then grated.

Then there are various meats, which must be lean and are served ground or finely minced, either cooked or raw. Heart is also used, boiled and ground and then added to mixtures.

Animal products also include milk: condensed milk can be served to some birds together with fruit juices and honey; dried milk can be added to food mixtures, etc. Hard curds are also good, but they must not be sour.

Insects and their larvae are another, special category of animal food. The commonest, eaten by both insectivores and other birds, are ant cocoons, either dried and added to mixtures or fed fresh. A good dried insect food consists of Mayflies, which every bird-keeper can catch on a summer night with light as bait. Mayflies are a suitable and good quality food and they cost nothing if caught by the bird-keeper himself. Also good are live bee larvae.

However, the most common live food is the mealworm, the name given to the larvae of various beetles of the family Tenegrionidae, and it can be fed to almost all birds. It is not difficult to breed this insect at home. The beetle and its larvae, however, occur in abundance in the wild, inhabiting barns with grain, granaries, bakeries and mills, and are also found in hen coops and even dove-cotes in the birds' excreta. The beetles can be kept in round, glass vessels but an improvement on these are shallow, wooden boxes with openings in the sides covered with wire mesh for ventilation. The bottom of such a box should be lined with perforated zinc, covered with a piece of jute sacking. On top is placed a wooden plate with food such as pieces of carrot, various vegetables, apple, egg, raw and cooked meat, for mealworms are omnivorous, dried carrot, Lucerne, groats and the like. The food should be changed twice a week. Besides the food vessel there should also be a shallow bowl with a piece of cotton soaked in water. The temperature in the box should be about 25° to 28°C. At higher temperatures the larvae grow more rapidly. The larvae hatch about three weeks after the female has laid her eggs (the exact time depends on the external conditions), then they moult ten or twelve times, after which they pupate and three weeks later the adults emerge, whereupon the cycle is again repeated. It is best to have several boxes for larvae of different sizes, so that it is possible to select the smaller ones for small birds. Some of the larvae are left to pupate for further breeding purposes. Hatched beetles can then be put in a new box where the females can lay their eggs, thereby continually renewing the bird-keeper's supply of fresh food. Some bird-keepers place the boxes one above the other in a cupboard. Before giving the mealworms to the birds it is advisable to sprinkle them with some mineral preparation so that the diet, particularly of young birds, is thereby certain to contain mineral substances plus trace elements and vitamins.

Excellent live food are crickets, which can likewise be reared by the bird-keeper himself. However, these are far more delicate. They must be kept at a constant temperature of about 28 ° to 30 °C and their breeding is more complicated and laborious. They, too, are kept in wooden boxes with glass lids. Each box should contain twisted pieces of paper to increase the crickets' overall living space. In the front part of the box a drinking vessel should be placed with water and a piece of cotton. The crickets should be given plant food (dried Lucerne, bran, oatmeal, grated carrot, etc.) as well as animal food (dried blood, ground boiled meat, etc.). A special section of the box should consist of narrow wooden compartments with finely sifted soil and sand where the females can lay their eggs. These containers are then transferred to a separate box where the young crickets hatch.

Some bird-keepers feed their birds maggots, which are the larvae of meat flies. Great care should be taken with these, however. Before feeding them to the birds, the larvae should be put in a layer of bran and sawdust to purge their digestive tracts. Otherwise the birds might die of poisoning. This is not a suitable food for beginners.

The most natural animal food is insects caught in the wild. Insects are easily captured by sweeping. The necessary equipment consists of a sturdy cloth sack on a strong round metal frame attached to a long handle and can be made by the aviculturist himself. This frame is swept from side to side over the grass and over the leaves of shrubs and trees and the contents of the cloth sack emptied every now and then into a tin with pierced holes for ventilation. Hornets and bees, however, should be released. Sweeping yields good quality food such as grasshoppers, flies, various hairless caterpillars, moths and beetles as well as a number of spiders. Before feeding the insects to the birds, the tin should be shaken sharply several times to stun them and prevent their running or flying away. Nevertheless, it is sometimes impossible to give such insect food to birds caged in an apartment for some of the insects are certain to escape, but it makes very good fare in outdoor aviaries.

Many birds may also be given silkworm larvae as they are not hairy. Likewise the ground meal of various sea crabs which contain many required nutrients.

VI MINERAL SUBSTANCES AND VITAMINS

These are supplied either in the natural state, e. g. Cuttlefish bones, ground eggshells, lime, or in special commercially sold mixtures.

Vitamins most often added to the bird's diet are Vitamins A, D, E, which are also present in young shoots and yeast, and Vitamin B. Some commercial food mixtures already contain the most important vitamins and trace elements.

VII SAND

Though not exactly a food, sand is important for almost all birds in helping pulverize food in the stomach.

VIII WATER

This is an extremely important part of the diet. Drinking water must always be fresh and not too cold.

IX FOOD MIXTURES

Insectivorous birds are fed various food mixtures, of which there are many, and every experienced bird-keeper prepares them according to his own recipes. However, the basic mixtures must be supplied without fail. Some of these are listed below.

Mixture for insectivorous birds: dried Mayflies or other insects, dried ant cocoons, a small quantity of liquid honey, shrimp meal, fish meal, finely ground or scraped lean meat, either raw or cooked, grated hardboiled egg, grated carrot, a very small quantity of vitamins, mainly A and D (one drop per small bird twice a week at the most, for an overdose is dangerous), some mineral substances and some fine breadcrumbs to keep the mixture crumbly. Some aviculturists recommend the addition of a minute quantity of scraped, unsalted bacon or a minute quantity of lard. Fat in the diet prevents feather plucking in some species. To this mixture may be added chopped mealworms or chopped crickets or grasshoppers; this is good fare for feeding caged birds in the home, for the insects cannot escape. On occasion even fresh curds can be added to the mixture.

The so-called 'Nightingale' mixture contains finely chopped cooked heart, grated hardboiled egg or egg biscuits as some bird-keepers recommend, grated carrot, ant cocoons, a minute quantity of ground hemp seed, and some mineral substances. Mealworms can also be added to the mixture. A recipe for egg biscuits is as follows: one half kilogram (one pound) of plain flour, six eggs and milk are combined to form a firm dough. This is then kneaded and rolled out into thin, round cakes which are baked until half done. After a few days they are then ground and added to the food mixture.

Another fine mixture for insectivores is: two parts grated carrot, one part ant cocoons, one part chopped mealworms, one part ground hemp seed, one part grated hardboiled egg, one part boiled lean meat or heart, one half part grated fresh curds, plus enough breadcrumbs to make the mixture crumbly and not cake.

A mixture for larger insectivorous birds, the so-called 'Thrush mixture' is as follows: two parts grated carrot, one part ant cocoons, one part ground boiled lean meat or heart, one part ground hemp seed, one part grated hardboiled egg, one part dried, crushed berries, plus enough breadcrumbs to keep the mixture crumbly. Some curds, dried Mayflies or other insects, shrimp and even Lucerne meal may be added to this mixture.

Many bird-keepers naturally improve on these mixtures and occasionally add other items to vary the diet of their birds.

NESTING AND PREPARING FOR NESTING

During the nesting period birds should be disturbed as little as possible. Some will abandon their eggs and leave the nest if disturbed frequently, whereupon the eggs get chilled and the embryos die. An occasional check, however, is sometimes necessary, but only with birds that will tolerate this.

The nests of birds, especially the small species that the aviculturist knows hatch and rear their young well, should be inspected as infrequently as possible, and best of all not at all. The only thing to watch out for is whether the parents return to sit on the eggs when they leave the nest, if they feed their young regularly, etc. However, there is no need to be hasty. Before the young hatch the adult birds sometimes leave the nest for as long as several hours, but with no harmful effects. Eggs should be removed only when the parent birds refuse to sit on them and, in the case of rare, exotic species, they should be put under some other bird to be hatched. Before doing so, however, they should be inspected by light to determine whether the embryos are still alive. Many birds abandon eggs with dead embryos and it would be a waste of time to place such an egg under another sitting hen.

In the case of some birds, especially parrots, it is important to check the eggs after about seven days to determine whether they are fertilized or clear. Parrot eggs are white and without any colour pattern, so that they are easily checked by light, the red veins of the growing embryo being clearly visible beneath the shell, which is not the case in eggs of a different colour. The red veins are branched and clearly and sharply outlined. There are no veins in a clear unfertilized egg, which should be removed from the nest so that the birds do not sit on it needlessly. Whether or not an embryo is dead can be ascertained by the red veins which in a dead embryo are irregularly branched, the shape of an indistinct circle or partial circle without the blastodisc. Such eggs should likewise be removed because they might burst and soil as well as choke the pores of the remaining eggs. Both clear eggs and ones with dead embryos may burst, if not earlier on then at the time of hatching, thus soiling the nest as well as the young birds.

A light-ray apparatus for checking the eggs can easily be made. The simplest is a plain box with a light bulb inside and an opening in the top fitted with a piece of rubber on which the egg can be placed. The eggs should be examined in the dark with only the light from the bulb shining through so that the veins will be clearly visible. A dark cover thrown over the head and shoulders and over the box will do. Since the eggs of various species differ in size, the opening in the box must be adapted accordingly, or else several openings of differing sizes should be made in the lid. In such a case all except the one being used should be covered when checking the egg.

Some birds, especially songbirds (e. g. Canaries), sit on the nest from the moment the first egg is laid. In this case, each egg should be removed until the whole clutch has been laid, and then the lot put back at one and the same time. While outside the nest the eggs should be kept in a cool room at a temperature of about 15 °C, but one that is not too dry. The eggs should be placed in their natural position, i. e. on the side, on slightly dampened sawdust mixed with sand and should be turned at least once a day.

For most species of exotic birds in captivity the aviculturist should prepare a nesting box. Birds nesting in tree hollows in the wild can be persuaded to nest by hanging up a suitable box. One advantage of this is that the bird-keeper can thus regulate their nesting and limit it to only as much as is suitable for them.

Nesting boxes are either natural ones made of the hollowed trunks of various trees, or artificial and made of wood. All nesting boxes should have a roof that lifts up so that the inside can easily be cleaned and inspected. Some species of birds prefer nesting boxes that are placed lengthwise, others ones that are deep. Birds kept in an aviary, where there is more space, can be supplied with various types of boxes from which they can take their choice. Many pairs are choosy and will not nest in a box they do not consider suitable. The kind of nesting box best suited for the given species is described in the latter part of this book which deals with individual birds.

Deep nesting boxes are usually furnished with a hinged door in the lower part to allow for easy inspection of the nest, removal of an egg, dead bird, and the like. It is best, however, to disturb the birds as little as possible during the nesting period and when necessary to do so only when the bird itself has left the nest. Never should it be removed forcibly. Species that are sensitive to any interference should be checked as little as possible, and only when absolutely necessary from some concealed spot, so as not to frighten them. Care should be taken to refrain from any noise during the nesting period, for the birds could become so frightened by it that they might fly out of the nesting box, dash against the wire netting of the cage or aviary and be killed. Strangers should likewise be kept away from the vicinity of the nest, for these, too, may frighten the birds who are well acquainted with the movements of their owner and members of his family, as well as the sound of their voices, and may find those of strange people disquieting. Never should a cat or any other animal be allowed near the nesting birds.

Songbirds, which build their nests in bushes or on the branches of trees, can be supplied with a ready-made nest, which many birds will adopt as their own. Such a nest can be either a small basket or else an abandoned bird's nest, say that of a Blackbird, finch or the like. Such a nest, which has already served to raise a family, must first be thoroughly cleaned, however. The best method is to sterilize it with steam, which will destroy any possible parasites or disease germs. The nest should then be dried and left to the birds, who will adapt it to suit themselves.

Some birds will not nest even if they are kept in pairs. These are gregarious birds that nest only in larger colonies and the aviculturist should therefore keep several pairs together.

Pairing birds, especially in the case of certain species of parrots, is sometimes rather a difficult task. Every bird-keeper prefers to pair unrelated birds, each from a different clutch. Young birds that have never nested are much easier to pair than older ones. Sometimes a bird that has lost its partner will obstinately refuse a new one, whereas another such bird will readily accept a new partner. It all depends on the individual:

Even young birds, however, should be paired some time before the breeding season, best of all in the autumn. Some species of birds, for instance certain parrots, often live together in pairs for as much as several years without nesting. Sometimes the female lays eggs that are unfertilized and only after three to five years does she hatch a young brood. In many instances patience is thus the prime requirement when pairing birds for nesting purposes.

DISEASES

The aviculturist who is acquainted with the behaviour of his birds in the wild state will easily recognize if something is wrong with any of them, if they are ill, etc. A sick bird is usually listless, perches in the corner of the cage, sometimes even on the floor, ruffles its feathers which are smooth and preened at other times, puts its head under its wing and sleeps much of the time. Also it does not react to a person's presence near the cage. Conspicuous symptoms are rapid breathing, markedly fouled feathers around the beak and mainly around the cloaca, and watery stools differing in colour from the excreta of a healthy bird.

Such differing, external symptoms do not immediately reveal the type of illness the bird is suffering from nor its cause. However, such a bird should be caught up at once and put in a special cage and another room to prevent the possibility of infecting the other occupants, should the disease be contagious. It is likewise necessary to clean the cage by replacing the perches, exchanging the sand, etc. and to disinfect it with a formaldehyde or peroxide solution. The plants should be washed, too, in addition to which they should be removed and kept a while in some other place.

There are many bird diseases and, therefore, only the most important ones are enumerated below.

TUBERCULOSIS. This disease, which is caused by the tiny *Mycobacterium avium*, is one that may be contracted by birds of all kinds. It is easily transmitted by the excreta of diseased birds as well as by the feeding, say, of eggshells that have not been previously boiled. The bird may also contract the disease from an afflicted human. Poor hygiene, insufficient fresh air and lack of enough sunlight are all factors that aid and abet infection. Birds contract tuberculosis generally through food, infection via the respiratory tract being less frequent. Such a bird begins to lose weight. This, however, is not evident at the beginning because of the coat of feathers and can be ascertained only by catching the bird in the hand. Furthermore, the bird continues to have a good appetite. Not until the advanced stage of the disease does the bird go off its food, ruffle its feathers, become listless and lethargic and sometimes have blood in its stools. Such a bird must be removed and isolated at once. When it dies it should be examined by a veterinary surgeon for the disease cannot be precisely determined by the aviculturist himself. Tuberculosis in birds is incurable.

The cage in which the diseased bird was kept should be disinfected with a three per cent formaldehyde solution or some other disinfectant, particular pains being taken that the hands are absolutely clean when doing so. The remaining, healthy birds should be given food rich in vitamins and minerals and their cage and surroundings should be kept immaculately clean. Those that were caged with the diseased bird should be isolated and kept under surveillance for a time to prevent any possibility of the spread of infection.

In some cases tuberculosis produces swelling of the joints and surrounding areas. Therefore, attention should be paid to the legs and also the wings, which droop. Sometimes a bird's death is caused by a ruptured liver as a result of tubercular infection. Tuberculosis is most easily recognised in the liver, which is enlarged and has small as well as larger white nodules. If the bird-keeper does not send a dead bird which is suspected of TB to be examined by a specialist, he should burn it. Under no circumstances should he have it stuffed because of the danger of further spreading of the infection.

PARATYPHOID. This is a frequent intestinal disease caused by the *Salmonella* bacteria and thus also known as salmonellosis. The type that occurs most often is caused by *Salmonella typhi murium* and can be transmitted not only to all other kinds of birds but also to mammals, including man. Young birds in particular are very susceptible to this disease, which in their case has a very rapid course. Adult birds may have salmonellosis a long time without any marked symptoms and only when they are in a weakened condition does the disease suddenly erupt. The bacteria can be transmitted by uncooked eggshells fed to the birds, inadequate hygiene, etc. The main carriers and main source of infection are mice and other rodents. Therefore every effort should be made to keep them away from the cage.

In the acute form the birds go off their food, have a low temperature and sit about on the floor of the cage. The stools are watery, whitish yellow or green and the area round the cloaca is markedly fouled. Sometimes there is a mucous discharge from the eyes, in other instances the birds fall from their perches and keep their balance with difficulty.

In the chronic form, especially in older birds, there is less activity at first, later lethargy and rapid loss of weight, which usually ends in death. Birds that recover should nevertheless be removed, for they remain carriers of the disease. If there is any suspicion that it is a case of salmonellosis the excreta, or even the dead bird itself, should be sent to a veterinary surgeon for examination. Only then is it possible to take the necessary steps.

Treatment has not been entirely successful to date. Medicines used are antibiotics such as chloramphenicol and streptomycin or sulphonamides. The best course to follow is prevention — lengthier quarantine of newly acquired birds, keeping mice away and scrupulous cleanliness.

PSITTACOSIS AND ORNITHOSIS. These are extremely infectious diseases which may be transmitted even to man, in whom it manifests itself as an acute inflammation of the lungs. In parrots the disease is called psittacosis, in other birds ornithosis. Parrots may already be affected by it in the wild state and can easily infect other parrots when put together with them in a cage. For this reason the import of parrots captured in the wild should be subject to strict veterinary checks and is often much restricted.

The course of the disease is very rapid in the case of parrots. The bird goes off its food, sits about in a listless manner and ruffles its feathers. This is followed soon after by a watery stool coloured grey to grey-green, sometimes even dark green. The final stage is marked by disorders of the nervous system; the bird cannot keep its hold on the perch, loses its balance and soon after dies. In some parrots the disease evidences no outward symptoms and passes unnoticed, and such a bird can become a carrier. In a case like this it is difficult to spot the disease and even laboratory tests are often inconclusive. Diagnosis is also made difficult by the length of the incubation period, which lasts anywhere from five days to three months. The disease is transmitted to man generally by his inhaling infected air, but because of the rigid inspection of imported birds this disease is very rare in humans. Treatment of psittacosis has hitherto been unsatisfactory. The only effective measure is the preventive administration of antibiotics. Birds affected by the disease are generally doomed to die. Dead birds must be burned and those that were in the same cage must be destroyed as well. In handling new parrots during the quarantine period it is necessary to wear a face mask, lab coat and rubber boots, which must be removed on leaving the quarantine premises.

RESPIRATORY DISEASES. The most frequent and most common diseases of this group are the common cold and bronchial catarrh, usually caused by the bird becoming chilled, e.g. by a draught, which birds do not tolerate, a rapid drop in temperature, etc. When afflicted by a cold the bird's nasal openings are clogged and it breathes with difficulty, whereas in the case of catarrh the breathing is rapid. In such instances the birds should be isolated and put in a separate cage at a steady temperature of 35 ° to 40 °C, checked by means of a thermometer. This is achieved by partially covering the cage with a cloth and placing a lighted bulb immediately above it. The patient should be given nourishing food, rich in vitamins. Some aviculturists have a special hospital cage on hand for such occasions, which they usually build themselves. This is generally a box cage with air holes, a light bulb or other source of heat inside and a perch. The temperature can easily be regulated in such a cage as can the humidity, a very important factor for the sick bird. The clogged nasal openings should be cleaned and fine oil or diluted glycerine applied. As soon as the bird is its old self again, the temperature should be slowly and gradually lowered to normal. In more obstinate cases antibiotics prescribed by a vet are administered.

DISEASES OF THE DIGESTIVE TRACT. These may likewise be caused by a draught, chill, cold drinking water, spoiled food, etc. The symptoms are usually watery or mucous diarrhoea, coloured grey to grey-brown. The feathers round the cloaca are generally fouled and the bare skin reddish. The sick bird goes off its food and sits about in a listless manner. Such a patient should not be fed green or soft food and should be given weak camomile tea instead of water. The ambient temperature should also be raised. More severe cases are treated with antibiotics and sulphur drugs. The matted feathers round the cloaca should be cleaned with tepid water. In the case of constipation, on the other hand, the bird should be fed green food and a drop of oil may be put in the bird's beak or else a small bit of butter.

DISORDERS OF THE METABOLISM. This disease is called gout. The kidneys do not eliminate the salts of uric acid and these then accumulate in the kidneys and liver, as well as in the joints or below the skin, impairing the functioning of the affected organs. Treatment is very difficult. The food given to the bird must be low in protein. The disease is often accompanied by swelling of the wing and leg joints, and these may even be purulent. In the advanced stage gout is practically incurable and can be prevented only by a proper diet.

SHEDDING FEATHERS AND FEATHER PLUCKING. Birds shed their feathers regularly during moulting. The process is gradual, as a rule taking several weeks, with new feathers growing in to replace the old. This is particularly obvious in the male whose brightly coloured nuptial plumage is replaced after moulting by feathers resembling those of the female, or vice versa when he moults into his nuptial dress. During the moulting period, particular care should be taken to keep the cage clean, provide sufficient moisture, if necessary by spraying water with a spraygun, and adequate sunlight. The diet should also consist of more nourishing foods, insects, for instance, being a very important item. Peace and quiet are likewise important at this time for, if a bird is frightened by some noise or other and flies up against the wire netting, it can easily break the new, growing feather and bleed excessively.

It often happens that birds pluck their own feathers or those of their companions. Another form of feather plucking is the plucking of nestlings by their parents. As a rule this is caused by a lack of animal food in the diet. The obvious thing to do is to increase the amount of such food and perhaps even add a piece of unsalted bacon. Feather plucking, however, sometimes becomes a vice. In such a case the given bird should be isolated and attempts made to cure it of this habit, e. g. by giving it fresh twigs to nibble on, plus an increased dosage of animal food. Plucking of a bird's own feathers may also be caused by an overly dry environment, by lack of vitamins or minerals in the diet, or by feather or skin parasites. In some birds new feathers will grow in to replace the old, in others this is not the case and treatment is often very difficult, for the reasons may be several and neither vitamins nor minerals help put an end to this affliction. Sometimes improvement occurs only after several months. Shedding of feathers may also be caused by parasitic mites that suck blood, which causes itching of the skin and consequent rubbing of the spot with the beak. Such mites can be destroyed with DDT, with which the feathers should be carefully dusted, or some other preparation recommended by the vet.

CONJUNCTIVITIS. This generally occurs in newly imported birds and is caused by the conditions of shipment, usually poor hygiene or dust. Today, conjunctivitis is easily cured with antibiotics in the form of drops administered three times a day for about fourteen days.

RICKETS. This disease is caused by a lack of minerals in the diet, especially in the case of nestlings. The young have soft, curved legs and can barely manage to stand on their feet. The disease is treated by giving the birds mineral substances and vitamins, above all Vitamin D, for instance by sprinkling it on the food or on the insects fed to the birds.

DISEASES CAUSED BY PARASITES. The parasites that cause these diseases are divided into two classes, namely ectoparasites, living outside the body, and endoparasites, living inside the body of the host. Endoparasites are furthermore divided into intestinal parasites, those that invade the blood corpuscles and those that invade body tissues. The commonest avian disease of this type is coccidiosis caused by unicellular organisms living in the walls of the intestines and causing severe inflammation. It is an extremely infectious disease and spreads rapidly to the other birds in the aviary. The sick bird has a mucous, sometimes even bloody stool. Sulphur drugs are the recommended treatment, the dosage being determined by the vet after examination of the bird's excreta. Scrupulous cleanliness is a must.

Of the ectoparasites one of the commonest is the parasitic mite *(Chemidocoptes mutans)* which causes what is known as scabies of the leg. The mite burrows into the skin of the legs, causing scaliness. Treatment consists of applying oil or some other oily preparation to the affected spots, thereby keeping the air out and killing the mites.

Common intestinal parasites are worms, especially tapeworms, roundworms and small parasitic worms of the genus *Capillaria*. Tapeworms usually occur in imported birds; in captivity they have no intermediate host and do not spread to other birds. Roundworms, however, are another matter. Captive birds may be infected by these parasites, because roundworms lay eggs which are passed out with the excreta and find their way back into the digestive tract through fouled food. Parasitic worms of the genus *Capillaria* are tiny worms that burrow into the lining of the intestines. Their presence can be ascertained by laboratory examination of the excreta for eggs. Treatment is then prescribed by the vet.

Some very common ectoparasites belong to the Mallophaga group. They are small, flattened insects that feed on the scales of the skin and parts of feathers. They may, however, pierce the skin and feed on the blood. Should young birds be attacked by great numbers of these parasites, the result may even be death. Dusting with DDT or some such preparation is recommended as treatment.

DISEASES CAUSED BY BACTERIA. One of the commonest diseases in this group is that caused by the bacterium *Escherichia coli*, normally present in the bird's intestines, where it aids digestion. However, in the case of a poor diet or weakening of the bird's organism, the bacteria overmultiply causing illness, which may even result in death. Treatment consists of the application of antibiotics and sulphur drugs.

EGG BINDING. Difficulty in expulsion of the egg by the hen may be caused by several factors, for example sudden cold weather in the case of birds kept outdoors or lack of minerals in the diet. The hen is usually unable to expel the egg, sits about on the ground, ruffles her feathers and may sometimes even be unable to stand. The hen should be grasped with care, wrapped in a warm, damp cloth and placed above a vessel containing warm water. In more severe cases, expulsion of the egg may be assisted by carefully inserting an eyedropper in the cloaca and applying a few drops of oil to the egg. This, however, should be done only by an experienced bird-keeper, for the egg may easily be crushed inside the hen's body. Prevention, in this instance, is far the best method of banishing this affliction. In cold weather egg-laying hens should be transferred to warmer quarters; a heat source may be provided and the humidity of the cage should be increased.

There are naturally many more diseases and parasites than are mentioned here and it is therefore recommended that bird-keepers, especially novices, take their patients to an expert. Only a vet with a laboratory in which to perform the necessary tests can make an exact diagnosis and prescribe the correct treatment.

TALKING BIRDS

Man's desire to have a talking parrot goes back to the days of our great-grandfathers and maybe even before that. The parrot's ability to reproduce human words and even whole sentences brought it great popularity, but at the same time proved to be its misfortune. Parrots were captured in great numbers and exported from their native lands primarily to Europe. Having a parrot in one's home became the fashion of the day and most owners wanted nothing more of their pets than to have them talk. However, few were able to meet the exacting demands made on them. Even today many people think that when they buy a parrot he will start repeating everything they say to him as soon as they get him home. But it is not as simple as all that. Really good talkers are a rarity amongst parrots and such birds have always fetched a high price.

Not every parrot will learn to talk. Whether it does or not depends not only on the species but mainly on the ability of the individual to mimic other sounds than its own. The African Grey Parrot, for instance, is one of the most gifted, the Budgerigar very little. However, some Budgerigars have been known to learn more words than many an African Grey Parrot. Amazon Parrots, especially the Blue-fronted Amazon, are good talkers. Next come the parakeets, macaws and cockatoos. In almost every species there are individuals that have learned to reproduce words but their number is very small. Most parrots learn only a few words; the majority whistle only a melody and those that can say several words or even whole sentences are the exception. Such geniuses have a vocabulary of as many as a hundred words.

Teaching a parrot to talk requires infinite patience. A young bird, taken from the nest before it tries its wings or one that is tame and has no distrust of humans, provides the greatest hope of success. Such a prematurely-taken nestling must, of course, continue to be fed with an eyedropper for several days, a larger bird with a small spoon. The young bird should be fed a specially cooked mush of millet-grain or oatmeal to which is added milk, carrot juice and mashed, cooked egg yolk. After several days, soft ears of unripe maize, bits of fruit, etc., may be added to the mush. The young parrot should be taken up in the hand or on the finger and talked to several times a day. First and foremost, however, it must be isolated from all other birds, especially ones of the same species, so that it does not hear their natural vocal expressions. By the time it is three months old, when its powers of perception are already well developed, the bird will begin to show interest in the voice, or even the words that are being repeatedly uttered and which it is supposed to learn. The first words should be short and resonant. Gradually, more words are added. These are also used in short sentences having to do, say, with some common activity such as opening the door and the like. After a time the bird will begin to repeat the words and will remember them. Some parrots easily learn more words, whereas others only learn the first few. Some may even take as much as eight or more months before they learn to pronounce words.

Parrots, just like other higher animals, can be taught conditioned reflexes. Because parrots are without any doubt intelligent birds and are able to imitate certain sounds, especially human speech, conditioned reflexes may be very effective. No one is surprised to see a dog pull a string with his teeth and ring a bell, asking for a drink or to be let out. This is nothing more than a conditioned reflex, when the animal is given a regular reward for certain specific behaviour, even if the reward is nothing more than being let out for a run outdoors. A parrot, for instance, may say 'Polly wants a drink' and may really be thirsty. Of course, as in the case of the dog, the words here are a conditioned reflex and are uttered by the parrot as the result of long practised habit. In the same way the parrot's 'good evening' is a sound it has been intentionally taught to utter on a specific occasion, or rather impulse.

Parrots are not the only birds with the ability to mimic human speech. Others, too, have this talent and some learn to mimic other sounds by themselves in the wild state, a thing parrots cannot do as a rule. Such birds include the Common Starling. Stop and listen at the next opportunity when one starts to sing on the branch of a tree. All of a sudden the Starling squawks like a hen, which it hears often. And in late March you may hear the flute-like song of the Golden Oriole. How did that come to be here at this time of the year? The explanation is simple. It is not a Golden Oriole but a Starling giving an expert imitation of the song it heard the preceding year. The Starling is likewise excellent at mimicking various creaks, squeaks and other sounds.

One of the best known talking birds is the Mynah, a member of the starling family living in southern and southeastern Asia. Its imitation of the human voice is truly remarkable. This again, however, is true only of the occasional, gifted individual. Often it learns to say various words sooner than a parrot. Corvine birds such as the Raven, Jay, Magpie and Jackdaw likewise frequently learn to utter single words. Even the crow will sometimes learn a word or two. The Rook, on the other hand, learns words only rarely, though he is good at learning to whistle various tunes.

As we have seen, parrots are not the only birds capable of mimicking various sounds, words and even whole sentences. However, these have no meaning for them whatsoever in the sense that they have for man.

PLATES

CHINESE FRANCOLIN

(Excalfactoria chinensis) Phasianidae

This species is widespread in southeast Asia ranging all the way to Australia. It is one of the smallest of the gallinaceous birds, attaining a length of about 12 cm (5 in) and is one of those most easily kept in cages. The female is coloured brown with white bands on the head and breast and black horizontal bands on the sides of the body.

This bird lives in open country, in grassy and bushy locations, frequently in mountain regions. It feeds on small seeds, grass and leaves as well as small insects and molluscs. The nest is a scrape made in long vegetation. In the wild the hen usually lays four brownish eggs covered with dark spots; in captivity, however, she can lay any number from seven to twelve. The eggs are hatched only by the hen who sits from sixteen to eighteen days.

The Chinese Francolin should be kept in a larger cage, the floor covered with sand and moss. A piece of turf should also be put there for nesting. Newly hatched chicks are very small and can even squeeze through a 1.5 cm (less than an inch) opening. For this reason it is recommended that a band of fine, wire-mesh netting be stretched around the cage before the chicks hatch, to prevent their escaping. The young should be fed a protein mixture for poultry, ant cocoons, finely chopped egg mixed with carrot and milfoil plus a small amount of dried Lucerne and sifted breadcrumbs, so that the mixture is crumbly. Lettuce should not be given as green food for it causes diarrhoea in this group of birds. The diet should include a sufficient quantity of live insects, e.g. crickets and insects, obtained by sweeping. Mealworms are not given to the chicks before they are ten days old. Larger Chinese Francolins may be fed finely chopped nettles and small seeds such as millet, canary seed and flax seed. Adult birds may be given granulated food normally available in shops, but lightly crushed.

CALIFORNIA QUAIL

(Lophortyx californicus) Phasianidae

This quail inhabits the dry regions of the United States from southwest Oregon to California. In recent years it has been introduced to other parts of that country. It measures about 24 cm (10 in). The female has the top of the head coloured black-brown with a small crest and off-white throat, and the remainder of the plumage less brightly coloured than the male.

It nests under bushes, often near a large boulder, but it will even nest in a clear space in the grass. The clutch consists of twelve to sixteen cream-coloured eggs, covered with golden, sometimes brown, and chestnut spots and splotches. Captive birds nest well and lay about fifteen eggs. The hen sits on the eggs from twenty-one to twenty-three days. If the hen is expected to nest, it must be supplied with ample room. An aviary, which can be partially sown with grass and where it is possible to place several stones, is better than a large cage. The California Quail gets along well with smaller parrots and other species of birds.

Some captive hens lay as many as fifty or more eggs but only the first twenty are generally fertilized. Such a hen will not sit on the nest and therefore it is advised that the cock be removed to other quarters after she has laid the twentieth egg, so that she will not become unnecessarily weakened. The chicks should be fed an abundance of insect food, otherwise the diet is the same as for the Chinese Francolin. At the age of four weeks the young leave the nest and roost in the branches, and at the age of three months the males begin to acquire their adult plumage. The California Quail can already nest the following year.

ROULROUL

(Rollulus roulroul) Phasianidae

This species is widespread in western India and the Sunda Islands. It measures 27 cm (11 in). The female's plumage is the colour of green grass and she does not have a crest.

The Roulroul lives in pairs and outside the nesting period in smaller groups or families. It inhabits bushy sites on the margins of virgin forests, spending most of the time on the ground and roosting in the branches during the night. The diet consists of insects, worms and small molluscs as well as green leaves, berries and seeds. Unlike other gallinaceous birds it scratches the ground with only one foot.

The nest is a lined hollow beneath a shrub and the clutch is from four to eight whitish eggs, rather large in proportion to the hen's body. The hatching period is nineteen days and the young take to their wings and roost in trees when only twenty-five days old.

In captivity the Roulroul gets along well with other species of birds and the aviary may also contain, for instance, small species of parrots. During the nesting period, however, the individual pairs must be separated. An aviary with an abundance of greenery should be sprayed with water more frequently, for the Roulroul is accustomed to the damp climate of the tropical forests.

The young should be fed small insects, ant cocoons, a fine mixture of boiled egg with carrot, dried Mayflies or other insects and also a supplement of dried nettles or Lucerne and chopped milfoil, etc. (but not lettuce). Larger adult birds are fed small seeds such as millet, canary seed, grass seed, bits of fruit, egg mixture, and now and then whole insects. Green, and even granulated food for gallinaceous birds should be served regularly as well. Drinking water should be put in a shallow vessel with several flat stones on the bottom so that the small chicks will not fall in and get soaked.

BLUE-CROWNED PIGEON

(Goura cristata) Columbidae

This species inhabits the northwest part of New Guinea and adjacent islands. Both sexes have the same plumage and attain the size of a turkey hen, although the legs are shorter.

The Blue-crowned Pigeon spends the day on the ground in the thick forest undergrowth but at night flies up onto tree branches to roost. The large nest is made of twigs and branches in trees. The clutch consists of one white egg which the parents take turns in hatching, the same as other pigeon species, for a period of twenty-eight to twenty-nine days. The young remain in the nest thirty to thirty-six days, but after leaving it, they continue to be fed by the parents for another two months or so. These giant pigeons feed on fallen fruit, soft fruit and seeds as well as invertebrates (mainly molluscs).

Its size makes this species unsuitable for a cage. It requires a roomier aviary, best of all an outdoor one in summer, sown with grass and containing some shrubs or small trees. The basic framework of the nest, either of reeds or osiers, should be attached to a strong branch, even a dead one, so that the nest will be sturdy and firm. Blue-crowned Pigeons are kept in pairs, for during the nesting period the male is aggressive towards other species of birds, including smaller pheasants and might easily kill them with a blow of his wing.

The diet consists of various seeds, grain, maize, also granulated food to which spinach, lettuce, etc., may be added. Fresh fruit, cut into small pieces, should be included and in winter stewed fruit. Insects may be given on occasion. During the winter the Blue-crowned Pigeon should be put in quarters kept at room temperature.

BLEEDING-HEART PIGEON

(Gallicolumba luzonica) Columbidae

The Bleeding-heart Pigeon inhabits the wooded areas of the Philippine Islands of Luzon and Polillo. It measures about 25 cm (10 in) and both sexes have similar plumage — only in some instances is the crimson patch on the breast larger in the male. The diet consists of seeds and fruits as well as insects and other invertebrates. The simple nest is built in a bush or on the lower branches of a tree. The clutch consists of two white eggs which hatch after sixteen days. The young leave the nest after fourteen to fifteen days.

Captive birds should be kept in pairs either in a roomy cage or an aviary. The floor should be covered with a layer of sand which should be changed frequently, for the pigeon always scatters some of its food and later eats it from the ground. If the cage is not kept clean, fungi or parasites might find their way into the bird's digestive tract. Therefore food remnants should always be removed, together with the upper layer of sand, which is then replenished. Outdoor aviaries should be sown with grass and grain, and should also contain a thick bush to which the bird-keeper attaches a basket for nesting. Although the Bleeding-heart Pigeon is quite tame in captivity, it is easily frightened during the nesting period and frequently abandons the nest if disturbed. If this happens the eggs may be put under a sitting Collared Dove to hatch.

The Bleeding-heart Pigeon should be fed seeds, grain, germinating corn, spinach and lettuce leaves, etc. It likes pieces of apple or blueberries, Rowan berries, and the like. Occasionally, it can be given mealworms or other insects or an egg mixture with carrot and cocoons. In winter the birds should be put in heated quarters, kept at room temperature.

COLLARED OR BARBARY DOVE

(Streptopelia decaocto roseogrisea) Columbidae

This dove, originally from eastern Africa, has been bred in captivity for centuries and thus has practically become a native species. Even buff as well as white individuals have been bred and their colouring has become hereditary.

In the wild, the nest of small twigs and plant stalks is built in a tree or bush. The clutch is two white eggs that hatch in fifteen to seventeen days. Captive birds nest without any trouble even in an artificial basket in the home, where one pair can be kept in a roomy cage. In an aviary it is possible to have several pairs plus a few pheasants and the like. The parents are very painstaking in their care of the young, and it is for this reason that the eggs of rare dove species that lay eggs in captivity but neglect their young can be given to the Collared Dove to hatch. A bird reared in captivity from the time it is hatched becomes very tame and friendly and can be let out of the cage to fly about the room or even out of the window to stretch its wings.

The diet consists of various seeds as well as green food such as spinach, lettuce, dandelion, etc. Insects may also be added on occasion. Some captive doves like small pieces of boiled, lean meat, but this should not be given very often.

In winter the Collared Dove should be kept in a room where the temperature is at least 10 °C. Outdoors, the toes might easily suffer frost-bite in sub-zero weather.

MOURNING DOVE

(Zenaidura macroura) Columbidae

This species inhabits the southern United States, Central America and the West Indies, being especially abundant in Cuba. It occurs in forest clearings overgrown with underbrush and in bushes on the edges of woods or in the neighbourhood of water. It lives in pairs and outside the nesting season in small colonies. The nest of twigs and plant stalks is built in a tall bush and in the woods also on the branches of conifers. The clutch consists of two white eggs which hatch in fourteen to fifteen days. At the age of two weeks the young leave the nest but the parents continue to feed them for about twenty more days.

The Mourning Dove feeds chiefly on seeds but also likes the grain it finds in ploughed fields. Other foods include green shoots and leaves and an occasional insect or spider.

A pair of these birds can be kept in a roomy cage in the home; in the case of an aviary it is possible to keep several pairs together. For nesting purposes, a shallow basket woven of reeds, osiers and the like will suffice; often the dove will not even bother to line it. Outdoor aviaries, where pheasants can be kept along with the Mourning Doves, should be sown with grass and grain. These doves like to eat the green food and also hunt there for seeds and small invertebrates. Besides the standard seeds fed to doves, they may also be given the seeds of conifers and a few mealworms now and then.

In winter the Mourning Dove should be kept in a room with a temperature of at least 15 °C. During this period it is possible to keep several doves together in one cage.

DIAMOND DOVE

(Geopelia cuneata) Columbidae

The Diamond Dove, one of the smallest of all doves and only 19 cm (7½ in) in length, is widespread throughout most of Australia. The area around the eye is not as red in the female as in the male, but the sexes can be distinguished definitely only by the behaviour of the cock when he courts the hen. It lives in scrub country, generally near rivers. Here it builds its nest of thin twigs and stalks of plants in a bush or tree. The clutch consists of two white eggs that hatch in twelve to thirteen days. The tiny nestlings grow rapidly and leave the nest about twelve days later. The Diamond Dove seeks its food, small seeds and green leaves, mainly on the ground.

It breeds freely in captivity and there have even been reports of a single pair nesting as many as seven times a year. One pair should be kept in a cage 1 m (40 in) long, 80 cm (32 in) wide and 80 cm (32 in) high. Outdoor aviaries, however, are much better for this dove, because it has greater freedom there to move about on the ground, which is its favourite habitat. For nesting, the cage should be provided with a small basket, woven of rushes or even of wire netting which the doves themselves then line with fine plant stalks, dry grass and the like. These doves may be kept together with other small birds, but should be separated during the nesting period, for their companions are often inclined to tear their nests apart.

The diet consists of millet, grass seed, canary seed, niger seed, plus a regular supplement of green leaves such as spinach and chickweed.

In the autumn the doves should be transferred to a heated room, for the female is sensitive to cold.

CRESTED PIGEON

(Ocyphaps lophotes) Columbidae

The home of this pigeon is Australia, where it inhabits open country, chiefly in the vicinity of lakes and streams lined with bushes or sparse woods. The flat nest of dry twigs is built in a bush or in the branches of a tree and two white eggs form the clutch. The young hatch in sixteen to eighteen days. In the wild, the bird feeds on various seeds, sometimes descending in whole flocks on tilled fields, where it feasts on the grain kernels. It also likes small fruit, green plant leaves and the occasional insect or snail.

In the aviary, it will also build its simple nest of twigs, but welcomes a shallow basket attached to a branch or bush. A pair of these pigeons can also be kept in a larger cage, where they likewise frequently nest. In the cage, the Crested Pigeon is aggressive towards other birds but in an aviary it is possible to have a greater number. In captivity it nests practically throughout the year, even outdoors. It is a very hardy species and tolerates even European winters, so that it can be kept in an outdoor aviary permanently. The only necessary precaution is to provide it with a roof or some shelter in the case of inclement weather.

In captivity, the diet consists of millet, wheat, barley, rice, crushed dried peas or lentils, spinach, lettuce, dandelion leaves, grass and other green food. An aviary can be sown with grass and grain. The diet may occasionally be supplemented with several mealworms or other insects and in the autumn with blueberries, cranberries and the like. Pheasants can be kept together with these pigeons in an aviary.

NICOBAR PIGEON

(Caloenas nicobarica) Columbidae

The Nicobar Pigeon, remarkable for its long, sickle-shaped neck hackles and about the size of a domesticated pigeon, is widespread from Nicobar east to the Philippines, New Guinea and neighbouring islands. It inhabits woods or the bushy margins of woods. Out of the breeding season it occurs in small flocks which fly from one island to another in search of food, especially to those that have a large harvest of fruit. It eats soft fruit that has fallen to the ground as well as seeds, green shoots and leaves, insects and other small invertebrates. During the day it generally remains concealed in branches, emerging to forage for food in the evening. A colonial nester, the flocks often remain together even during the nesting period, building several nests of small twigs on one tree. Unlike most pigeons, the female lays only one egg, the young bird hatching in sixteen to eighteen days.

The Nicobar Pigeon is a popular cage bird but the aviculturist must have only one pair in a cage, for in a small space the male is aggressive towards others of its own and even different species. It tolerates only smaller types of pheasants.

The diet in captivity consists of larger seeds, berries, pieces of soft fruit, and in winter stewed fruit and the occasional insect. Regular supplements should include green food such as spinach, chickweed, green corn and the like.

The Nicobar Pigeon nests in captivity and thus should be provided with a larger basket attached to a bush in a shady spot. It is sensitive to cold and should therefore be transferred to a heated room for the winter.

GOLD AND BLUE MACAW

(Ara ararauna) Psittacidae

One of the largest of all parrots, attaining a length of 90 cm (3 ft), this bird inhabits the tropical part of South America from Panama to Bolivia. The sexes are alike in plumage and it is almost impossible to tell them apart. Macaws live in forests, where they fly from tree to tree in search of food — various fruits, nuts, seeds and green shoots. The hen lays her eggs — two white, glossy eggs being the usual clutch — in a hollow tree and hatches them herself. The young emerge after twenty-three to twenty-four days, but remain in the nest a long time, leaving the hollow of the tree only at the age of about three months, when they already have their full plumage.

The captive Gold and Blue Macaw will frequently nest and hatch young, but it sometimes takes a very long time, even several years, before matching a pair that will nest. The aviculturist who wishes to breed this species should provide the birds with a large, hollow tree trunk, an old barrel with a hole in the side or a box of strong boards measuring 1 m (40 in) in length, 60 cm (2 ft) in width and 80 cm (32 in) in height. The opening at the side should be either circular, about 25 cm (10 in) in diameter, or square. The floor at the back of the nesting box should be slightly hollowed so that the eggs will not roll out.

The diet consists of sunflower seeds, wheat, germinating grain, lightly boiled rice, unripe ears of maize, nuts, etc., plus a generous amount of green food such as spinach and dandelion leaves, and fruit, both European and tropical, stewed in winter. Some birds appreciate a bit of curd, lean meat and hardboiled egg on occasion. Twigs for the birds to bite on should be supplied regularly.

RED AND GREEN MACAW

(Ara chloroptera) Psittacidae

This large, gaudy parrot, measuring about 80 cm (32 in), makes its home in South America from Guyana to Brazil and Uruguay. It inhabits the tops of the high trees of the rain-forests. Though brightly coloured, it is nevertheless practically invisible amidst the lush green of the foliage. Both sexes are alike in plumage. Out of the breeding season, the macaws occur in flocks that range through the trees in search of food, mainly various fruits, berries and shoots. They also like nuts, cracking the shells with their strong beaks without any difficulty. Now and then they also eat soft fruit and seeds from the ground.

During the nesting season the Red and Green Macaws live in pairs. The nest is a large, deep hollow generally high up in the tree trunk. The clutch consists of two, sometimes (though rarely) three white eggs, and the young hatch in twenty-four to twenty-six days. They leave the hollow at the age of three months, their plumage already resembling that of the parents, though the tail feathers are shorter.

In captivity these macaws may be kept singly, even at liberty, in a special spot in the home or in a roomier aviary covered with strong wire netting, for thinner wires are easily cut by the bird's strong beak. A careful watch must also be kept on the beak when catching the bird in the hand (to trim its claws or file the beak) for it may cause serious injury.

Care and feeding of the bird in captivity are the same as for the Gold and Blue Macaw.

BLUE-FRONTED AMAZON PARROT

(Amazona aestiva) Psittacidae

The Blue-fronted Amazon is widespread in the forests of Brazil, Paraguay, Bolivia and northern Argentina. The sexes have similar plumage and individuals exhibit a variety of colouring. It lives in tree-tops, mainly in the vicinity of water courses. The nest is a hollow tree and three to four white eggs form the clutch, on which the hen sits for thirty days. The young become fledged at the age of sixty-five days or so and the birds then roam in families or together with groups of other fledglings. During the nesting period, adult birds live in pairs. The natural diet consists of various fruits, green shoots and seeds, which the birds seek in the tree-tops.

In captivity, the birds should be fed primarily sunflower seeds and a small quantity of hemp seeds. Also appreciated are unripe ears of maize. The diet should likewise include fruit, both native and tropical, and green food such as spinach, dandelion leaves and lettuce. In the winter months, the birds may be given stewed fruit, the branch of a fruit tree to nibble on, etc. An occasional mealworm or other larger insect is welcomed, and even a sausage now and then.

The Blue-fronted Amazon Parrot can be kept at liberty in the home, its allotted space being a corner of a room supplied with a branch and the floor beneath covered with a sheet of paper, metal sheet, etc. Some individuals do not leave their nook, whereas others fly about and these must be put in a larger cage for the night. In summer the bird can be put in an aviary which, if there is a pair, can be provided with a nesting box measuring 30 cm (12 in) in length by 30 cm (12 in) in width by 50—80 cm (20—32 in) in height, should the birds decide to nest; this, however, happens only rarely. This parrot is an excellent mimic and learns to talk well.

YELLOW-HEADED AMAZON PARROT

(Amazona leucocephala) Psittacidae

This beautiful bird is found in Cuba, the Isle of Pines and the Bahamas. It lives in pairs on the edges of forests or in dense brush with the occasional tall tree, in the top of which it spends much of its time, making forays into the neighbourhood in search of various fruits, berries, green shoots and various seeds. The Yellow-headed Amazon is also a frequent visitor of orange and banana plantations, where it eats the sweet ripe fruits. The nest is a hollow, generally high up in the tree, lined with a small amount of decayed wood. The clutch consists of two to five eggs. The young hatch after one month and are fledged two months later, but remain with the parents, who still feed them for a time. It is an interesting thing that the Yellow-headed Amazon is not in the least fearful or timid in the wild state.

In captivity its diet consists of various seeds, mainly sunflower seeds, unripe ears of maize and the like. Fruit, both native and tropical, e.g. orange or banana, should be provided regularly and also a fresh twig to bite on. In winter, stewed fruit can be given instead of fresh. Insects may be given on occasion, though some individuals refuse this, and also small amounts of spinach, chickweed, etc.

The Yellow-headed Amazon can be kept in a roomy cage or without any cage at all. It is quickly tamed and then constantly demands the owner's presence. It can also be taught several words.

UPPER YANGTSE PARAKEET

(Psittacula derbyana) Psittacidae

The home of this parakeet is southern China, North Vietnam and the island of Hainan. The male has a red beak, the female's is black. The Upper Yangtse Parakeet lives mainly in the thick tree-tops at the edges of forests in pairs, and after the nesting period roams about the neighbourhood in family groups. The nest is a hollow usually high up in a tree. The clutch consists of two to five eggs, on which the hen sits for twenty-two to twenty-five days. When the young are fledged after about six weeks, they all have red beaks, even the females. Within a month, however, the beaks begin to turn black and by the end of summer all the young have black beaks. Not till the following year do the males acquire permanent red beaks.

In the wild, this species feeds on seeds, berries, fruits, green shoots, unripe nuts and occasionally also insects.In captivity, the diet should include sunflower seeds, hulled oats, hemp seed, wheat and green food such as spinach, dandelion leaves, green corn. Fruit or willow twigs may be added now and then. In winter the birds should be given stewed fruit.

The Upper Yangtse Parakeet is kept in an aviary provided with a nesting box 25—30 cm (10—12 in) wide, 45 cm (18 in) high, with an entry hole about 10 cm (4 in) in diameter. The wooden parts of the aviary or large cage must be of hard wood or other sturdy material, for the birds nibble soft wood. The wire netting must also be of greater strength. Adults may be kept outdoors throughout the year, even in winter, as they are very hardy. However, they should be provided with a box for shelter. Young birds should be taken inside for their first winter.

PLUM-HEADED OR BLOSSOM-HEADED PARAKEET

(Psittacula cyanocephala) Psittacidae

The Plum-headed Parakeet, reaching a length of 35 cm (14 in) — a large part being taken up by the long tail — inhabits India and Ceylon. The female has a greyish head, a yellowish band on the throat and no red patch on the wing. The young are similarly coloured. In captivity, one sometimes comes across the yellow form (lutino).

This species lives in forested areas, mainly on the margins of woods, whence small flocks descend on nearby fields. The nest is a hollow, high up in the tree where the female lays four to six white eggs on which she sits for twenty-one to twenty-three days. The young leave the nest at the age of forty-two days, being able to fly immediately.

Captive birds can be kept in pairs in large cages of an overall length of 1 m (40 in) by 60 cm (24 in) wide by 80 cm (32 in) high. But even better is an aviary where the pair can also nest. The nesting box should measure about 17 × 17 cm (7 × 7 in) by 30 cm (12 in) high with an entry hole 5 cm (2 in) in diameter. The hollow may, however, be even deeper. If one wants the birds to nest, it is advisable for the pair to be put in an outdoor aviary for the summer, where they have more sunlight and greater freedom of movement.

The diet consists of various seeds, sprays of unripe grass and ears of unripe grain, an abundance of fruit such as apples and oranges, and in winter stewed fruit and a bit of tomato on occasion. When feeding the young, the diet should be supplemented with mealworms, which the parents give the nestlings. Insects should be sprinkled with mineral substances and even vitamins before being fed to the birds. Another good supplement at this time is a grated, hardboiled egg, combined with grated carrot and ant cocoons. An occasional budding twig of a fruit tree is also welcome.

RING-NECKED PARAKEET

(Psittacula krameri) Psittacidae

There are two races, the Indian *(Psittacula krameri manillensis)* inhabiting India, Ceylon and part of Burma, and the African *(Psittacula krameri krameri)* inhabiting tropical Africa. The latter is rarer in captivity, is somewhat smaller and the beak is more chestnut-red. The females of both species are without the black and pink ring around the neck.

The Ring-necked Parakeet lives on the margins of forests, whence it ventures in small flocks into fields in search of grain. It also feeds on fruit for which it goes farther afield to more distant plantations. The nest is a tree hollow and the clutch consists of four to six white eggs on which the hen sits for twenty-two to twenty-three days. This species may be kept in pairs in roomy cages or aviaries. The cage should be at least 1 m (40 in) long, 60 cm (24 in) wide and 80 cm (32 in) high. The birds, however, prefer to nest in an aviary which should be at least 1,5 m (5 ft) long, 1 m (40 in) wide and 1.8 m (6 ft) high. The more roomy the aviary the better. The nesting box should be about 20 × 20 cm (8 × 8 in) and 30—40 cm (12—16 in) high with an entry hole about 8 cm (3 in) in diameter. If a natural hollow trunk or branch is used the inside may be even larger.

Feeding and general treatment in captivity are the same as for the Plum-headed Parakeet but the bird-keeper may add more sprouting twigs (from willow or fruit tree) as well as germinating corn.

The Ring-necked Parakeet has several colour varieties bred in captivity, e. g. yellow (lutino), white (albino) and even blue.

ROSEATE COCKATOO OR GALAH

(Kakatoe roseicapilla) Psittacidae

This bird inhabits a large part of Australia. Both sexes are alike, except for the eyes, those of the male being dark, almost black whereas those of the female are usually dark orange-pink. The length is about 35 cm (14 in).

The Roseate Cockatoo is a gregarious bird that roams the countryside in flocks, separating into pairs only for the nesting period, when it seeks out hollows in dead gum trees, lining the nest with the freshly plucked leaves of that tree. There are four to five white eggs in the clutch. In their native land these flocks of Galahs, as they are called, cause damage in cornfields and are mercilessly persecuted by farmers.

In captivity, this bird is hardy and undemanding. It can be kept in a roomy cage or aviary. Lone specimens that have been tamed can be allowed to fly about freely in the home, but should be put in a cage for the night. In the summer it is recommended that an outdoor aviary is provided with a nesting box measuring 40 × 40 cm (16 × 16 in) and about 1 m (40 in) high. If it is deeper, a ladder should be affixed to the wall to allow for easier entry and exit. The Roseate Cockatoo, however, rarely nests in captivity, though when it does the birds are exemplary parents.

The cage diet consists of sunflower seeds, a small amount of hemp seed, hulled oats, germinating corn, nuts, etc. Sweetened milk, which the birds like, may be given on occasion. There should likewise be an abundance of green food such as spinach, chickweed and dandelion leaves, plus clover blossoms, the shoots of fruit tree twigs, fruit, both native and tropical, and in winter, bits of stewed fruit. In autumn Rowan berries and the like provide welcome variety.

ROSELLA PARAKEET

(Platycercus eximius) Psittacidae

The home of this parakeet is the eastern part of Australia, where it occurs in three races. The male is usually more vividly coloured. The hen lays four to nine white eggs in a hollow branch and sits on them by herself for twenty to twenty-two days. In captivity, some hens lay even more than thirty eggs, but then as a rule refuse to sit on them. As in the case of other parrots, the male feeds his mate during this period and also helps to feed the young. The nestlings leave the nest at the age of one month, but continue to be fed by the parents for a further three weeks or so. The Rosella Parakeet sometimes produces two broods in a season. For nesting, captive birds should be provided with a nesting box at least 25 × 25 cm (10 × 10 in) and 35 cm (14 in) high and with an exit 8 cm (3 in) in diameter. Deeper boxes, about 80 cm (32 in) deep, are better but these should have a ladder attached to the inside wall. Adequate moisture is a must for otherwise the eggs would dry out, and the best way to ensure this is to make several holes in the bottom of the box and stand it on a bowl of water or damp moss.

The cage for Rosellas should be about 2 m ($6\frac{1}{2}$ ft) long, 60 cm (2 ft) wide and 1 m (40 in) high and the nesting box should be attached on the outside. Even better is an aviary where adult birds may be kept outdoors throughout the year, for they are very hardy.

The diet is simple, the staple foods being sunflower seeds, millet, canary seed, hulled oats and hemp. The birds should also be given an abundance of fruit and fruit tree, willow or Hazel twigs. During the nesting period, but also at other times, insects are added, as well as grated hardboiled egg, together with carrot and ant cocoons. When grass becomes ripe, the diet should include sprays of grass, unripe ears of corn, maize, etc., and a regular supplement of green food.

STANLEY PARAKEET OR WESTERN ROSELLA

(Platycercus icterotis) Psittacidae

This species inhabits south Australia, where there are two races. The female has smaller yellow patches on the cheeks and is less brightly-coloured than the male. The young are a greenish hue and moult after two months, but do not assume full colour until after one year.

The hen usually lays six to eight eggs in tree hollows, sitting on them for twenty to twenty-two days, during which time she is fed regularly by the cock. She only leaves the nest now and then to stretch her wings. The young leave the hollow after one month.

The Stanley Parakeet is one of the smallest of the Rosellas and may therefore be kept in a roomy cage indoors. An aviary, however, is better for nesting: one measuring 2 m (6½ ft) in length, 1.5 m (5 ft) in width and 1.8 m (6 ft) in height is quite adequate. The birds should be kept in pairs. Nesting boxes best suited for this species should be about 80 cm (32 in) deep. If kept in an outdoor aviary this should be sown with a mixture of grasses, whose seeds the birds like and which they feed to their nestlings. Ornamental shrubs may also be planted there and nesting boxes hung in their shade. A shallow bathing pool with water will be more than welcomed by the occupants. Some aviculturists leave the Stanley Parakeet outdoors even in winter, but this is not advisable. Young birds should be kept in a heated room for their first winter.

Pairing this species is sometimes rather difficult. Best of all are young individuals that have not yet nested; older specimens are harder to pair. The best method is to let them get acquainted while each is in a separate aviary or with another cage in between, for instance. Stanley Parakeets can be kept together with other small birds.

PENNANT'S PARAKEET OR CRIMSON ROSELLA

(Platycercus elegans) Psittacidae

This bird is widespread in Australia from north to south, where it occurs in six races, which differ often quite markedly in the colouring of the plumage. Frequently the two sexes are exactly alike. In their first year, many young birds are entirely green, whereas others already have the characteristic plumage as soon as they are fledged. However, full colour is not assumed until the autumn of the following year. (N. B: sometimes young green birds are sold as females!)

Pennant's Parakeet frequents woods and shrub country. It often goes about in large flocks, is fearless and often does great damage to grain fields. The nest is a tree hollow and the clutch consists of four to nine white eggs. The hen sits on them for some twenty to twenty-two days as a rule. In captivity she lays eggs with fair regularity, but often will not sit.

This species is one of the larger parakeets and therefore not suited to a cage. It should be kept in an aviary, best of all an outdoor one, though an indoor one will do almost as well. It must, however, be made of hard wood for the Pennant's Parakeet likes to nibble soft wood and could escape through the hole it makes. It should be supplied with an abundance of twigs for this purpose and the wire netting should be of thicker gauge.

Feeding and general treatment are the same as for the Rosella Parakeet; however more insect and egg food should be provided when the parents are feeding nestlings. In captivity the Pennant's Parakeet is a peaceable bird and fairly hardy. Nevertheless, it is recommended that the bird be taken inside for the winter and kept at room temperature; a lower temperature will do no harm but care must be taken to avoid draughts.

GREEN PARAKEET OR GREY-BREASTED PARAKEET

(Myiopsitta monachus) Psittacidae

This is a common bird in Argentina, Paraguay and Bolivia, where it occurs in great numbers. The sexes are alike and difficult to tell apart. It lives in great flocks and is also a colonial nester. Unlike most parrots, it does not nest in a tree hollow, but builds a huge, round, communal nest of twigs in tall bushes or tree-tops where each of several pairs, sometimes as many as twenty, has its apartment. Four to six eggs form the clutch and the young hatch in twenty-five to twenty-six days. They leave the nest at the age of forty days but remain members of the colony. The diet consists of seeds, fruits and green shoots.

In captivity the Green Parakeet can be kept singly or in pairs in a roomy cage indoors, though an outdoor aviary is preferable. This need not be large and allows several pairs to be kept there together. Furthermore, the birds breed well in such an aviary. The bird-keeper can attach an old basket or board below the roof and supply willow, poplar or other twigs as nesting material, leaving the birds to build the nest themselves. The birds are more easily paired if kept in greater numbers.

The Green Parakeet should be fed sunflower seeds, millet, hemp, hulled oats, ears of corn, as well as germinating grain, broken grain mixture, fruit and a regular supplement of twigs with young shoots.

It is not recommended to keep more than one or two specimens indoors, as these birds are very noisy. Being very hardy, however, they may be left outdoors even in freezing weather, but must be sheltered from winds.

PATAGONIAN CONURE

(Cyanoliseus patagonus) Psittacidae

This species inhabits the southern parts of South America. Both sexes have similar plumage and it is hard to tell them apart. It lives in partially wooded, rocky locations, usually in pairs, and after the nesting period, in families and small flocks. The nest is a tree hollow or rock wall fissure. The usual clutch is two to three white eggs and the young hatch in twenty-six days. The diet consists of various seeds, fruits, green shoots, buds and the occasional insect.

Captive birds should be kept in a roomy cage with strong wire netting, though an aviary is preferable. This need not be particularly large. For nesting purposes it should be provided with a hollow tree trunk, preferably about 1 m (40 in) deep, or else a man-made hollow of hard wood with a ladder attached on the inside to facilitate the bird's exit and entry.

The Patagonian Conure will eat practically everything it is given. The diet should consist primarily of sunflower seeds, hemp seeds, wheat, etc., with an occasional unripe ear of maize or wheat. Good supplements are twigs of fruit, willow and other trees, and during the nesting season also an egg mixture. Green food such as spinach, dandelion leaves and grass should be supplied regularly, and in winter, green corn which can be made to germinate in a box in a warm room. A piece of stewed fruit provides welcome variety.

The Patagonian Conure is very hardy and adults may be kept outdoors throughout the winter. However, they should be provided with a shelter to which they can retreat.

AFRICAN GREY PARROT

(Psittacus erithacus) Psittacidae

This parrot, which attains a length of some 35 cm (14 in), inhabits the forests of tropical Africa. The sexes have similar plumage, but the male has a more massive skull and larger beak.

Out of the nesting season it congregates in flocks, otherwise it lives in pairs. The eggs, usually two white ones, are laid in a large tree hollow and the young hatch after thirty days. Not until they are seventy days old do they abandon the hollow.

In captivity they are lethargic, sitting for long hours in one spot, and can thus be kept at liberty in the home, a strong branch on a firm base being all that is necessary. However, a suitable cage is one that measures about 50 cm (20 in) in length, 30 cm (12 in) in width and 40 cm (16 in) in height. If one wants the bird to nest, it should be put in an aviary provided with a nesting box, 25 cm (10 in) square and 50 cm (20 in) high, with an entry hole 11 cm (4½ in) in diameter. A natural hollow may be even deeper. However, this species rarely nests in captivity.

The caged bird should be fed sunflower seeds, hemp, wheat, hulled oats, nuts, groundnuts, unripe ears of maize, etc. Germinating grain is likewise good, especially in winter. The diet should also include carrot, spinach, lettuce and the twig of a fruit or willow tree now and then, as well as European and tropical fruits. Mealworms, a piece of hard-boiled egg or sausage may be provided occasionally for variety. Cooked food is not suitable fare.

The African Grey Parrot prefers shade and should not be put in an open, sunny spot. Young captive birds readily learn to imitate various sounds and words, are easy to tame and very affectionate.

BUDGERIGAR

(Melopsittacus undulatus) Psittacidae

The home of this species is Australia where most specimens are coloured green. However, many colour forms have been bred in captivity and more are being added. The male is distinguished by the blue colour round the nostrils, which area is brown in the female.

Budgerigars should be kept in pairs in cages about 60 cm (24 in) long by 40 cm (16 in) wide by 40 cm (16 in) high, or else several pairs together in an aviary. They are more likely to nest in greater company. The nesting box should be about 15 cm (6 in) square and 20—25 cm 8—10 in) high with an entry hole 4,5—5 cm (1½—2 in) in diameter. Boxes placed lengthwise with the opening to one side are also good. The clutch usually consists of three to six and sometimes as many as twelve white eggs, the hen often sitting as soon as the first is laid. The young thus hatch successively after a period of eighteen days, and are fledged at the age of thirty to thirty-five days. When parents are caring for the young the birds should be fed an egg mixture with carrot and ant cocoons or dried Mayflies or other insects, with added mineral substances, eggshells or Cuttlefish bones. Adults should be given millet, hulled oats, a little hemp seed, green food such as spinach, dandelion leaves and unripe ears of wheat, plantain heads, and the like. Soft twigs of fruit trees covered with buds may be provided occasionally. Some specimens like a piece of apple, but fruit is not their natural diet.

Budgerigars are very hardy and if provided with a shelter can be left outdoors in mild winters.

PETZ' CONURE

(Aratinga canicularis) Psittacidae

The home of this bird, which measures about 25 cm (10 in), is Central America and Mexico. The sexes are alike. Petz' Conure frequents the margins of forests or bushy locations and tall stands of cacti, where it frequently also nests. Otherwise the nest is a tree hollow. During the nesting period it occurs in pairs or even in colonies. Out of the breeding season, it ranges the countryside in flocks searching for food which consists of the seeds of grasses and other seeds, berries and shoots as well as fruits, for which it visits plantations.

A flock of these birds may even be kept in captivity, in an aviary, of course, which should be provided with several nesting boxes more than the number of paired birds. An aviary measuring 3 × 2 m (10 × 6½ ft) and 1.8 m (6 ft) high can hold as many as five pairs at a time. Single specimens or one pair may be kept in a cage in the home, but this should be roomy enough to allow for flight. The nesting boxes should be 17 × 18 × 30 cm (6½ × 7 × 12 in) high but may be as large as 25 cm (10 in) square and 35 cm (14 in) high, with an entry hole 6 cm (2½ in) in diameter. The hen sits on the eggs for twenty-three to twenty-five days, during which time she is fed by the male; frequently he also sleeps by her side at night. The young leave the nest at the age of forty-five to fifty days, when they already resemble their parents, though they are not as vividly coloured.

Petz' Conure is not hard to feed and is content with sunflower seeds, millet, canary seed, plus sprays of millet, grass, etc. Green food such as spinach and dandelion leaves should be a regular part of the diet, also an occasional piece of fruit and in spring, fresh fruit-tree twigs and germinated grain. In winter, the bird should be kept in a heated room.

BLUE MOUNTAIN LORIKEET OR RAINBOW LORIKEET

(Trichoglossus haematodus) Psittacidae

This bird inhabits Australia and neighbouring islands all the way to the Lesser Sunda Islands. It measures 30—35 cm (12—14 in) and there are several races. Both sexes are alike, the male being distinguished by the more massive skull. The hen lays two white eggs in a nest built in the hollow of a eucalyptus tree. The incubation period is twenty-three to twenty-six days and the young are fledged at the age of eight weeks or so. They resemble the parents, except for the beaks, which are dark. After the nesting period, they range the countryside in huge flocks, occurring chiefly in eucalyptus woods, where they feed on the nectar of blossoms. They also eat soft fruits and sometimes even insects and greenstuff.

Captive birds require a special diet that substitutes for the nectar they feed on in the wild. This consists of sweetened corn starch pudding, sweetened milk and a little fruit syrup, juice of stewed fruits, etc., plus honey. Soft tropical and continental fruits may also be provided; in winter stewed fruits. During the breeding season, the birds should be given a daily ration of mealworms, which the parents feed to the nestlings, also grated hardboiled egg with carrot and ant cocoons and now and then some green corn, spinach, etc.

The Blue Mountain Lorikeet may be kept in a smaller indoor or outdoor aviary; a pair may also be kept in a larger cage. Non-nesters may number several to a cage, but a nesting pair should be given a cage to themselves. The nesting box should be 20 cm (8 in) square and 80 cm (32 in) high, and the entry hole should measure 10 cm (4 in) in diameter. Three weeks after fledging, the young should be transferred elsewhere so that the mating pair can rear a second brood. In summer the aviary should be sprayed lightly with water; in winter the birds should be placed in heated quarters.

CRIMSON LORY

(Domicella garrula) Psittacidae

Several races of this species are widespread in the Moluccas, where they roam in small flocks. The sexes are alike and it is hard to tell them apart. The nest is a tree hollow, usually in the vicinity of water. The clutch consists of two white eggs and the incubation period is twenty-five days. The young remain in the nest about eight weeks and are fed by the parents for two or three more weeks after fledging. The Crimson Lory likes soft fruit, such as oranges, and often raids plantations. It also feeds on the nectar of blossoms and occasionally also on insects and green shoots.

The diet in captivity is the same as for the Blue Mountain Lorikeet — milk puddings, fruit syrup, soft tropical as well as European fruits, and during the breeding period also insects, egg mixture and bits of spinach, lettuce, etc.

This robust bird is kept one pair to a cage measuring about 1.5 m (5 ft) in length, 1 m (40 in) in width and 80 cm (32 in) in height. An aviary, of course, is even better. The nesting box should be about 30 cm (12 in) square, 80 cm (32 in) high with an entry hole 12 cm (5 in) in diameter. The bottom of the box should be arranged to form a shallow hollow, several holes should be bored in the wood and a vessel with water or damp moss placed underneath to maintain the required moisture inside, especially on hot summer days, so that the eggs cannot dry out. Both indoor and outdoor aviaries should be sprayed with tepid water in the summer; the same should be done indoors in the winter months when the birds are in a heated room. The Crimson Lory is less likely to nest in captivity than the Blue Mountain Lorikeet.

ECLECTUS PARROT

(Lorius roratus) Psittacidae

Several races of this species make their home in New Guinea, northern Queensland (Australia) and the Moluccas, Aru and smaller neighbouring islands. The plumage of this 45 cm (18 in) bird is markedly different in the male and female, so much so that they were originally believed to be two distinct species. The cock is coloured a bright green whereas the hen is a magnificent red.

The Eclectus Parrot can be kept in a smaller indoor aviary and in summer in an outdoor one; however, the pair should have it to themselves. The nesting box should be made of hard wood for soft wood is easily damaged by the birds' beaks. It should be fairly large, best of all 35 cm (14 in) square and 1 m (40 in) high with an entry hole 12—14 cm (4½—5½ in) in diameter. The inside wall should be fitted with a ladder and a vessel with water or damp moss placed underneath the bottom.

The diet differs from that of lorikeets but is the same as for larger parrots, namely an abundance of green food and fruit, both European and tropical, sunflower and other seeds, germinating grain, some curds and in summer unripe ears of maize, etc.

The Eclectus Parrot soon becomes acclimatized in captivity and is not disturbed by the presence of humans. When the hen sits on the eggs, however, the male is very aggressive towards all intruders and the hen, though she will not leave the eggs, makes good use of her strong beak, pecking at anyone who comes near. The nest should be checked for possible broken eggs only when she leaves it.

TURQUOISINE GRASS PARAKEET

(Neophema pulchella) Psittacidae

At one time very widespread in eastern and southern Australia, this bird is now rare and found only in New South Wales. The female differs from the male in that it lacks the red shoulder patch and the blue colouring is not so vivid.

This parakeet lives in wooded areas where it feeds on the ground. The nest is a hollow where the hen lays four to nine white eggs, sitting on them as soon as the third egg has been laid. The incubation period is nineteen to twenty-one days and the hen alone feeds the young until they are fledged, which is usually after twenty-eight to thirty-two days, whereupon they are fed for a further ten to fourteen days by both parents.

The cage for this bird should be at least 75 cm (30 in) long, 50 cm (20 in) wide and 50 cm (20 in) high. Even if kept in an aviary, which is more suitable for these birds, one pair should have it to themselves, for the Turquoisine Grass Parakeet is very aggressive during the nesting period. The nesting box should be about 17 cm (7 in) square, 25 cm (10 in) high or even more, with an entry hole 5 cm (2 in) in diameter. As soon as the young are able to fend for themeselves, about fourteen days after fledging, they should be put in a separate cage or aviary as the male frequently attacks the young females and, besides, the pair is usually preparing to raise another brood.

The diet consists of millet, canary seed, hulled oats, sunflower seeds, etc., and regular rations of spinach, dandelion leaves and chickweed. In winter a little crushed hemp seed may be added and sometimes also thistle seeds. During the breeding period, besides the staple diet the bird should also be given an egg mixture with carrot, ant cocoons and mineral substances. In summer, outdoors as well as indoors in a warm room, the cage should be sprayed with tepid water.

COCKATIEL

(Nymphicus hollandicus) Psittacidae

The home of this species is the interior of Australia, where it lives in bush and woodland country. The female is less brightly coloured than the male. A nomad, the Cockatiel is found in large numbers wherever there is an abundance of food. The nest is a hollow in a tree. The hen lays five to seven white eggs and, unlike most other parrot-like birds, the parents take turns sitting on them. The young hatch after twenty-one days and are fledged after three to four weeks.

Captive Cockatiels have several broods a year. A pair can easily be kept in a cage indoors. This should measure about 1 m (40 in) in length, 50 cm (20 in) in width and 70 cm (28 in) in height. In an aviary, it tolerates the company of other birds. For breeding, the Cockatiel should be provided with a nesting box about 25 cm (10 in) square and 30—35 cm (12—14 in) high, though it may be even deeper, with an entry hole 7—8 cm (2 ½—3 ½ in) in diameter. The floor of the box should be hollowed out and filled with a layer of soft wood shavings. A branch may be attached outside the entry hole for the birds to perch on.

In the wild, the Cockatiel feeds mainly on various seeds, also insects and the nectar of eucalyptus blossoms. In captivity, the diet should consist of various grass seeds, wheat, sunflower seed, unripe ears of grain, also millet, canary seed, hemp and other seed. The Cockatiel will appreciate an occasional bit of fruit, both European and tropical. When the adults are feeding their young, the diet should also include egg mixture with carrot and an added supplement of dried Lucerne, mineral substances and even vitamins. Spinach, dandelion leaves, some Lucerne, lettuce or other green food should be provided throughout the year. The Cockatiel is a hardy bird and, if provided with a shelter, can be kept outdoors even in winter.

PEACH-FACED LOVEBIRD

(Agapornis roseicollis) Psittacidae

This species, measuring about 15 cm (6 in), is one of the most beautiful of the lovebirds, and makes its home in southwest Africa. The sexes are alike in plumage. In the wild, it breeds in the nests of weaver-birds. The clutch consists of four to six white eggs, sometimes even more. The incubation period is twenty-one to twenty-two days and the young leave the nest when they are about thirty-five days old, returning there, however, for the night.

In captivity, the Peach-faced Lovebird breeds commonly in wooden nesting boxes 15 cm (6 in) square and 30—35 cm (12—14 in) high, with an entry hole 5 cm (2 in) in diameter. The box may be even larger. It should always be hung in the shade and a bowl of water placed underneath to maintain the necessary moisture inside. Before nesting, the cage or aviary should be provided with an abundance of twiggy branches of willow or poplar. The hen peels the bark from these twigs and uses it to construct her own nest inside the box. She does this by herself, as a rule, the male helping only on occasion. The nest is round and firm, but sometimes, however, it has only a front and side wall.

In captivity, Peach-faced Lovebirds should be kept one pair to a cage at least 70 cm (28 in) long, 40 cm (16 in) wide and 50 cm (20 in) high. An aviary is even better and in this the aviculturist may keep several pairs provided, however, with a sufficient number of nesting boxes.

The Peach-faced Lovebird should be fed various seeds, green shoots, spinach, dandelion leaves and for variety the twiggy branch of a fruit tree or willow, a piece of apple, etc. In summer, it can be given unripe ears of grain or plantain heads. In winter, the birds should be taken indoors and kept at room temperature.

MASKED LOVEBIRD

(Agapornis personata) Psittacidae

This species makes its home in Tanzania and Malawi. The male and female are alike and it is difficult to tell them apart. The nest is a tree hollow, which the female lines with small twigs and peeled bark, carried there in her tail feathers. In captivity, twiggy branches should be provided during the nesting period so that the birds can peel off the bark for their nest. The female usually lays four to six white eggs. The incubation period is twenty-one to twenty-two days and the young remain in the nest until the age of thirty-five days.

This member of the parrot family can be kept in pairs in larger cages and in summer in an outdoor aviary, which gives the birds more opportunity for exercise. Likewise, they breed more often in an aviary. The nesting box, either a ready-made one or a hollow branch (the latter being preferable) should be hung in the shade. The Masked Lovebird likes to bathe and the cage or aviary should be provided with a shallow bowl of tepid water.

The diet consists of various seeds such as millet, canary seed, hulled and unhulled oats, hemp seed, sunflower, also unripe sprays of grass and ears of grain as well as green twigs. These birds do not like fruit but will eat a bit of apple now and then.

A blue variety of this species has been bred; it is very popular but as yet comparatively rare. The young if taken from the nest before fledging and fed by the bird-keeper are quickly tamed and very affectionate to their owner.

RED-HEADED LOVEBIRD

(Agapornis pullaria) Psittacidae

The Red-headed Lovebird inhabits tropical Africa. The female's face-mask is yellow, whereas the male's is vermilion, and her under-wing coverts are green. Nesting takes place in the hollows of trees or in the nests of tree termites where the bird burrows tunnels, terminating in a nesting chamber. The clutch is five to seven white eggs.

Its unusual nesting habits made this bird unpopular with most aviculturists for it used not to breed in captivity and shied away from nesting boxes. Today, however, it is a common cage bird in England where it also nests freely. Moss is placed in the nesting boxes and these lovebirds burrow tunnels in this, laying eggs in the chambers at the end. The tunnels look very much like mouseholes.

When first imported the Red-headed Lovebird is very delicate, but young birds reared in captivity thrive and are hardy. Some specimens have even become adapted to their new environment and line empty nesting boxes with grass and bits of straw. The birds prefer a box laid lengthwise, for it is more reminiscent of a termite nest. The box should be hung in the shade.

The diet is the same as for other lovebirds. It can be supplemented with tropical fruit, but this is not necessary. Much appreciated are unripe ears of maize, also heads of wheat, oats, plantain and the like. Grass may be grown in the aviary, which may likewise be sown with grain or millet. In winter the birds should be kept in a heated room.

WHITE-CHEEKED TOURACO

(Tauraco leucotis) Musophagidae

This species occurs in two races in Ethiopia, Somaliland and southeast Sudan. The total length is 45 cm (18 in) and both sexes have the same plumage. In Africa, it is called the Banana-eater, because of its fondness for that fruit. However, it also eats other soft fruit and likewise berries. Variety is provided by the occasional insect or other invertebrate and by green shoots. It lives in pairs and out of the breeding season in families. The nest, a fairly large but not very sturdy construction, is made of twigs and located high in the tree-tops as a rule. The hen lays two to three whitish or greenish eggs, which both sexes take turns hatching. The young are fed food regurgitated by the parents. It is interesting to note that the young remain in the nest for only ten days or so and leave it before they are capable of flight, merely venturing out on branches, where the parents continue to feed them.

The White-cheeked Touraco presents few problems in captivity, but requires an abundance of food. The diet consists of pieces of fruit, cherries, etc., whole, and stewed fruit in winter, sliced vegetables, hardboiled egg with grated carrot, green food and an occasional insect or larvae. Chopped or minced meat may be given now and then. It must always be provided with a larger bath, for this is something the Touraco is inordinately fond of. For nesting, a large basket or plaited nesting box should be hung high up in the aviary, always in the shade. This is lined by the birds themselves — with willow twigs and stalks. Touracos, however, breed infrequently in captivity. In winter, the birds should be transferred to a heated room.

GREAT HIMALAYAN BARBET

(Megalaima virens) Capitonidae

The home of this bird is Burma and southern China. The sexes are alike in plumage and the total length is about 32 cm (12 in). It frequents the margins of forests, the vicinity of forest clearings, and the like. A very active and sprightly bird, it is usually to be found in the tree-tops where it seeks its food. The diet consists of insects and their larvae, soft berries and fruits. The nest is a tree hollow where the hen lays some two to four white eggs. The incubation period is thirteen to fifteen days and the young when they hatch are blind and without feathers. Both parents sleep in the nest at night and one of the partners uses the tree hollow even out of the breeding season.

The Great Himalayan Barbet poses few problems in captivity. It should be kept in a larger cage or preferably an aviary, especially in the case of paired birds, for the male is very aggressive in a small space, even towards his mate out of the breeding season. For this reason, it is recommended that only single specimens be kept in a small space.

The diet consists of a 'Thrush' mixture with egg, carrot and ant cocoons or dried Mayflies or other insects, also pieces of boiled lean meat, pieces of fruit, diced, boiled carrot, green food such as spinach, dandelion leaves, lettuce, etc., various berries and on occasion live insects, e. g. mealworms and crickets.

The cage or aviary should be provided with a nesting box, either a natural tree hollow or made of boards, in which the Great Himalayan Barbet generally sleeps. Captive birds breed with difficulty. The male has a monotonous but melodic and fairly pleasant voice, which it uses quite frequently. The Great Himalayan Barbet will live for many years in captivity.

TOUCO OR GIANT TOUCAN

(Ramphastos toco) Ramphastidae

This bird is one of the largest of the toucans, attaining a length of 60 cm (2 ft). The sexes are alike and difficult to tell apart. The Touco frequents the rain-forests of Guyana and Brazil, where it lives in the tree-tops, descending to the ground only for the berries and fallen soft fruits it eats. In the trees it moves about with short hops. It is a good flier, but only for short distances. The natural diet is composed chiefly of soft, juicy fruits and berries, as well as insects and small vertebrates the bird catches adroitly with its huge beak. It takes nestlings of other birds from the nest and also catches small lizards, as well as other reptiles and amphibians. The nest is a hollow in a tree, sometimes almost at ground level, at other times high up. The clutch consists of two to four white eggs and the parents take turns incubating them for sixteen days. The young remain in the nest for six to seven weeks and are fed chiefly fruit juices by the parents.

The diet in captivity is by no means difficult, though it is somewhat different from the usual foods and must be supplied in greater quantities. It is composed of boiled rice and pieces of fruit; cherries and other small fruits may be given whole. In winter, stewed fruits plus hardboiled egg with grated carrot, boiled potato, etc., should be given. Insects, a small mouse or sparrow should be provided as an occasional supplement.

Toucans cannot be kept together with other smaller birds for they would kill them. Therefore it is advisable to keep them in pairs in a larger aviary, which should be provided with water in a bowl, for these birds are very fond of bathing. In captivity the Touco easily becomes acclimatized and is very affectionate.

CHESTNUT-BILLED EMERALD TOUCANET

(Aulacorhynchus haematopygus) Ramphastidae

The Chestnut-billed Emerald Toucanet inhabits the northern regions of South America, where it lives at higher elevations in the rain-forests, in small flocks or families and during the breeding season in pairs. The sexes are alike in plumage. It feeds chiefly on various soft fruits and berries, partly also on insects and their larvae, and on occasion other invertebrates as well as small vertebrates such as lizards. At night, it retreats into the hollows of trees, one hollow sometimes containing several birds. It sleeps in the typical posture of toucans, with the beak tucked into the feathers on the back and the tail feathers raised up above it. They sleep like this even in captivity on a branch, if not provided with a box. Like other toucans it makes its nest in a tree hollow but, unlike the former who leave remnants of food in the nest, Chestnut-billed Emerald Toucanets keep theirs immaculately clean. The hen lays two white eggs which hatch after sixteen days.

Because of their smaller size they may be kept in a larger cage, though they breed there only rarely.

The diet should comprise various fruits cut into small pieces, in winter, various stewed fruits, boiled rice plus berries such as blueberries, Rowan berries, etc., for variety. A few mealworms are a welcome supplement now and then. The birds should also be provided with a larger bowl with water for bathing. The floor of the cage or aviary should be cleaned daily and covered with fresh sand. Birds kept outdoors should be taken inside in the autumn and put in a heated room. In captivity, individually kept specimens soon become tame and affectionate.

PERUVIAN COCK-OF-THE-ROCK

(Rupicola peruviana) Cotingidae

The range of distribution of this species extends from the northern Andes and Colombia to Peru, where it frequents mountain regions with open spaces, chiefly in the vicinity of streams and rivers. Rocky locations are where it is generally to be found and it is here that it also performs its courtship display. The dance is performed by one male at a time, while the other birds look on. The female has dark, red-brown plumage and the total length is 35 cm (14 in). The nest is made in a rock crevice and is somewhat reminiscent of the swallow's nest, for it is constructed of mud and twigs and lined with leaves. The birds get along well together and sometimes nest in colonies. The clutch comprises two greyish-yellow eggs covered with red-brown spots. The incubation period is nineteen days. The Peruvian Cock-of-the-Rock feeds on insects and their larvae, also worms, snails as well as fruits and soft berries and feeds its young with insects and fruit.

In captivity, the aviculturist may keep one specimen in a larger cage or a pair in an aviary. These are peaceable birds and the aviary may contain plentiful greenery, for they do it no damage. The diet should include various soft fruits cut into small pieces, e.g. bananas, oranges, pears, apples, apricots, as well as strawberries, cranberries, blueberries and the like. Live insects should be provided regularly. Because of its huge appetite and consequently its large quantity of excreta, which is liquid as a result of its eating fruit, greater effort is required in keeping its quarters clean and tidy. The floor is best covered with a layer of sand with which the excreta are then easily raked out. Water should be supplied in a shallow bowl.

EASTERN FLYCATCHER

(Tyranus tyranus) Tyranidae

The Eastern Flycatcher is widespread in North and South America. The total length is about 20 cm (8 in). It likes to nest in orchards, in tall trees, and is usually found in the vicinity of rivers and streams. The nest is of twigs, stalks, dry grass, wool, etc., and is lined with feathers, horsehair, wool or other soft material. The hen lays three to four white to pale pink eggs with chestnut spots. The diet consists chiefly of various insects and spiders, and in lesser part of soft fruits and berries and only occasionally small seeds.

In captivity, it should be in a larger cage which a pair of birds have to themselves. Other birds cannot be housed with this species even in an aviary. The Eastern Flycatcher is very aggressive, even towards stronger adversaries and in the wild state will even attack crows and kestrels and chase them off, which in view of its small size is a truly remarkable feat. It is powerful in flight, however, and can thus afford such daring. The diet in captivity consists of the 'Nightingale' or 'Thrush' mixture with a regular ration of live insects and larvae, and also fresh ant cocoons. Juicy fruits, e. g. an orange cut in half crosswise, and in winter stewed fruit should be supplied as well. The Eastern Flycatcher likes to bathe and will welcome a shallow bowl filled with tepid water. In summer it can be kept in an outdoor aviary, but only with such birds as pheasants, which it will not attack.

GARNET PITTA

(Pitta granatina) Pittidae

This species is widespread in Malaysia, Borneo and Sumatra. Both sexes have similar plumage. It spends most of its time on the ground where it moves with short hops, usually in the thick undergrowth of the jungles. The nest, a globular structure of twigs, roots and leaves lined with fine wool, fibres and hairs and with an opening at the side, is built in the undergrowth either on the ground or just above it. The clutch consists of three to four mat, white eggs covered with red-brown to violet spots and patches. The Garnet Pitta is primarily an insect-eater but also eats small snails or worms which it likewise seeks on the ground.

In captivity, the Garnet Pitta may be kept in a larger cage measuring about 1.5 m (5 ft) in length, 50 cm (20 in) in width and 60 cm (2 ft) in height. This, however, must be provided with a 'jungle' inside, which can be made of reeds as well as tall grass to make it feel at home. Moss and sand is a good floor cover. In a cage, however, the male may sometimes attack the female, for it is primarily a lone bird out of the breeding season, and it is best to keep a pair in an aviary, where there is more undergrowth for the female to hide in. This species is difficult to breed in captivity and thus is generally kept singly and not in pairs.

The diet consists of insects, such as mealworms, crickets and locusts and should include a regular ration of the 'Thrush' mixture plus an occasional piece of cooked, lean meat. The Garnet Pitta lives long in captivity and in an aviary will tolerate several other bird families, e. g. the Fringillidae.

SOUTH AMERICAN JAY

(Cyanocorax chrysops) Corvidae

This popular cage bird makes its home in southern Brazil, Uruguay and Paraguay. The total length is 37 cm (15 in) and both male and female have similar plumage. Out of the breeding period, these birds roam the countryside in small flocks and during the nesting season they live in pairs. The nest of dry twigs is built in tall, preferably thorny trees. It is a haphazard affair, lined with roots, bits of grass, hairs, etc. The hen lays six to seven bluish eggs and the young hatch in seventeen to eighteen days. In the wild state, it feeds on various insects and spiders and often raids the nests of other birds, taking both eggs and young nestlings. It likewise catches and eats amphibians and even small reptiles, though the diet also includes plant food such as berries, green shoots and larger seeds.

In captivity, it should be kept in a larger cage or preferably an aviary, but otherwise it poses few problems. It will eat almost anything it is given — bits of meat, leftovers from a meal, even boiled potatoes, chopped vegetables, curds, fruit and, of course, insects, though the latter are not a must. When the nestlings are being fed, the diet should be supplemented with insects and egg mixture with carrot and ant cocoons. The South American Jay breeds frequently in captivity and should be provided with a basket lined with some dry grass and moss, which the bird then completes by itself. Individual pairs should be kept separately during the breeding period, but otherwise several specimens can be put in one cage. A single cage bird kept by itself is easily tamed and can be allowed to fly about the room.

GREEN MAGPIE

(Cissa chinensis) Corvidae

The Green Magpie inhabits the territory from the Himalayas to southeast Asia, and spreads all the way to Borneo and Sumatra. The total length is about 35 cm (14 in) and both sexes have similar plumage. The nest of dry twigs, lined with roots, blades of grass, etc., is built in a tree or tall bush. The clutch usually comprises three to five greenish, brown-spotted eggs and the incubation period is eighteen days. After the young have been fledged, these birds congregate in families or small flocks. The diet consists of various insects and their larvae, small vertebrates, especially young birds, which the Green Magpie takes from the nest, soft fruits and occasionally seeds. In the Himalayas, the natives remove young Green Magpies from the nest and train them to hunt small birds.

This species of bird is not recommended as a cage bird and if kept in a cage then only singly, and in one that measures at least 1.5 m (5 ft) in length. Much the best is an aviary containing a thick bush and long branches for a pair of these birds.

In captivity, the Green Magpie should be fed pieces of cooked or raw meat and insects, and as a supplement chopped vegetables and curd, hardboiled egg, etc. It welcomes a small sparrow or mouse now and then. In winter, the bird should be put in a heated room at room temperature. It may be kept together with larger species of pheasants, but not during the nesting period when the latter might take their eggs from the nest.

BLACK-NAPED ORIOLE

(Oriolus chinensis) Oriolidae

This species is widespread in India, southeast Asia and the Sunda Islands. The female is not as vividly black on the head and her chin is whitish, but an older specimen sometimes is no different from the male. The Black-naped Oriole is found in pairs on the edges of jungles, especially in river valleys and even at higher elevations. It generally frequents the dense tree-tops where it conceals itself perfectly. The nest, built about 2—5 m (6½—16½ ft) above the ground on the terminal branches of trees, usually in the fork, is of fibrous grasses, bast and other materials which are flexible and can easily be woven into a basket-like nest; it is sturdier than the nest of the Common Oriole of Europe but otherwise of the same shape. The hen lays three to four pinkish eggs covered with rust or ash-grey spots. The young hatch in fourteen days. In the wild state the Black-naped Oriole feeds mostly on insects and their larvae, also spiders and sometimes soft fruits and berries.

Captive birds should be kept in a larger cage at least 1 m (40 in) long, 40 cm (16 in) wide and 60 cm (24 in) high. An aviary, however, is better (an outdoor one in summer) for the bird does not have the required exercise in a cage and is apt to get fat. The diet consists of the 'Thrush' mixture with hardboiled egg, grated carrot, ant cocoons and also frequent rations of live insects or larvae such as mealworms. Good supplements are pieces of fruit, even tropical fruit, and in winter stewed fruit.

The Black-naped Oriole rarely breeds in captivity and then only in a large aviary. Confined birds change colour after a time.

RED-WHISKERED BULBUL OR RED-EARED BULBUL

(Pycnonotus jocosus) Pycnonotidae

This bird occurs throughout India and southeast Asia especially in the mountain regions. The female has a smaller red ear patch and shorter crest, but otherwise the sexes are alike. The total length is 20 cm (8 in). The nest of roots, dry grass, stalks, leaves, wool and the like, is built in dense undergrowth or in a tree-top, chiefly by the female, the male often helping by bringing her nesting material. The clutch is usually only two to three eggs. The young hatch in twelve days and are fledged twelve days later, the parents continuing to feed them for a time. The diet is primarily insects and berries.

The bird may be kept singly in a cage about 80 cm (32 in) long, 50 cm (20 in) wide and 60 cm (24 in) high. A breeding pair should be kept in a larger cage. An aviary may contain other birds of about the same size, but the Red-whiskered Bulbul is aggressive to others of its kind. These Bulbuls breed in captivity, sometimes rearing more than one brood. If kept in an outdoor aviary, this should contain a bush, where the birds can build their nest.

The diet consists of the 'Nightingale' mixture, various insects such as mealworms, grasshoppers and also small crustaceans. Live food is a must for these birds. The diet may be supplemented by soft fruits, the occasional berry and bits of green food.

The Red-whiskered Bulbul is quite hardy (in the wild state it often lives in mountain regions), but it should be taken inside for the winter and kept at room temperature.

GOLDEN-FRONTED LEAFBIRD

(Chloropsis aurifrons) Chloropsidae

This species attains a length of 20 cm (8 in) and inhabits southeast Asia. The female resembles the male but has less black on the crop. The young are greenish without the orange patch on the forehead. Nesting takes place in dense foliage. The clutch usually consists of three whitish eggs with dark, red-brown spots. The incubation period is twelve days. In the wild, the diet comprises various insects and their larvae and the nectar of blossoms. The birds often visit flowering gardens and likewise plantations, where they suck the sweet juice of ripe fruits.

In captivity a pair may be kept in a cage that is at least 80 cm (32 in) long, 50 cm (20 in) wide and 60 cm (24 in) high. The birds require roomier quarters because they are very active, and will welcome a branch covered with thick foliage. In an aviary, they may be kept together with other birds — members of the finch family for instance — but there should be only one pair of Golden-fronted Leafbirds as the males of this species do not tolerate one another.

It needs to be given warmth, and though it may be kept outdoors in summer it should be taken inside for the winter. Newly imported birds require a liquid diet such as diluted fruit juice combined with milk and honey, orange juice, various soft fruits and small insects. Later they may be given strawberries and grapes and, in winter, stewed fruit. They will also eat the 'Nightingale' mixture with egg, carrot and ant cocoons. Soft fruits should be provided throughout the year.

PEKIN ROBIN

(Leiothrix lutea) Timaliidae

The Pekin Robin is widespread in northern India, Burma, southern China and Vietnam, where it frequents the shrubby growths near woods and also gardens. The sexes are much alike in plumage, the male being distinguished by his song. The nest of dry stalks, hairs, feathers, moss, pieces of paper and other material is built in dense thickets. The hen usually lays some three to four whitish eggs covered with red-brown spots and streaks. The parents take turns incubating them, the female usually sitting at night. The young hatch after twelve days, and when they have become fledged the parent birds prepare to raise another brood. The natural diet consists of various insects, soft fruits and berries.

In captivity, the Pekin Robin should be kept in a larger cage or aviary; in the latter it may also have other birds as companions. During the nesting period, however, the pairs should be housed separately for they pluck the feathers of smaller birds to line their nest. The aviculturist can provide them with a woven basket and plenty of feathers, hairs and soft moss to line the nest. The diet consists of the 'Nightingale' mixture, soft fruits and insects. The Pekin Robin is especially fond of oranges cut in half crosswise. Small quantities of small seeds may be given now and then and also a bit of green food such as spinach, lettuce, chickweed and the like.

A hardy bird, it tolerates our climate quite well, even the cold, and some bird-keepers in coastal regions leave it outdoors even in winter, though this is not generally recommended. The Pekin Robin when reared in a cage from its early youth soon becomes tame and can be allowed to fly freely about the room.

WHITE-CRESTED JAY THRUSH

(Garrulax leucocephalus) Timaliidae

This bird inhabits the Himalayas and its distribution extends from there all the way to southern China, Taiwan and Sumatra. The sexes are alike in plumage and attain a length of about 27 cm (11 in). It frequents wooded, mountain areas where it can be found in thick bamboo stands. The nest is of dry stalks and bamboo leaves, lined with fine, dry grass, moss and hairs. The clutch as a rule comprises only three bluish-green eggs. The White-crested Jay Thrush feeds on various insects and other small invertebrates as well as fruit and berries in the wild state. Sometimes it raids the nests of other birds and devours the nestlings, though this is not a regular habit.

Captive birds may be kept in a larger cage, at least 1.5 m (5 ft) long, provided with several branches, on which they are fond of hopping with long hops. In summer it may be put in an outdoor aviary together with other species which, however, should be more or less of the same size, for it is aggressive towards smaller birds. Smaller species of pheasant may also be included in the aviary. The White-crested Jay Thrush does not breed in captivity.

The diet consists of a 'Thrush' mixture, plus an occasional supplement of pieces of lean meat and live insects. It is fond of soft fruit, especially tropical fruit, but will be satisfied with European varieties and in winter stewed fruit.

It is very hardy, but in winter should be kept in a room that can be heated and kept at a temperature of about 10 °C. Single specimens reared in a cage in the proximity of man rapidly become tame and are very amusing.

RED-LEGGED THRUSH

(Mimocichla plumbea) Turdidae

This species makes its home chiefly in Cuba and the Bahamas. The total length is from 24—26 cm (10 in). The sexes are alike in plumage, but the male can be recognized by his song, which is pleasant but monotonous. The nest, built in a thicket or occasionally in a semi-hollow, is made of roots, stalks, hairs, etc. The clutch consists of three to five greenish-blue eggs and the incubation period is thirteen days. The young are hatched only by the female and leave the nest at the age of twenty days, being fed by the parents for another two weeks. The diet consists chiefly of insects, berries and fruit.

It breeds well in captivity, mainly in roomy, outdoor aviaries, where a pair may be kept together with smaller species of pheasants. Out of the breeding season, more than one pair can be housed together. Two weeks after they have become fledged, the young should be put in another cage or aviary in order that the cock does not attack them when the pair begins raising another brood.

Cage birds should be fed a 'Nightingale' mixture, plus a regular ration of insects and larvae as well as sweet fruits, stewed in winter. The Red-legged Thrush will welcome even small pieces of cooked lean meat. Green food should be supplied throughout the year. When it is feeding its young it should be provided with more plentiful amounts of insects. Mealworms should be dusted with mineral substances before being fed to the birds. Hairless, silkworm caterpillars as well as insects caught by sweeping are a good supplement.

This bird may even be kept singly in the home in a roomy cage. Specimens kept outdoors during the summer should be taken inside into a heated room for the winter.

SHAMA

(Copsychus malabaricus) **Turdidae**

The Shama inhabits the forested areas of India, Ceylon and southeast Asia, chiefly in the vicinity of rivers, occurring also in city parks and gardens. The female is predominantly olive-brown and has a shorter tail. The total length is 24—26 cm (10 in). The nest is built in a thicket, generally of bamboo, and sometimes in holes, by the female with the male assisting — he brings her straw, dry grass, roots, wool, etc., with which to build. Four to five dark green eggs with brown spots form the clutch and the young hatch after eleven to thirteen days. The female is fed by the male while she incubates the eggs and the young are fed primarily by the hen, though the male also brings food. By the age of one month the young are able to fend for themselves. In the wild state the Shama feeds on various insects, berries and soft fruits.

Captive birds should be kept in a larger cage, an outdoor aviary being recommended for the summer, where they breed well. When old enough the young should be removed so that the parents can start raising another brood.

The cage or aviary should be provided with a large shallow dish with water for bathing and should be sprayed now and then with tepid water to keep the air moist.

The diet in captivity consists of the 'Nightingale' mixture with egg, carrot and ant cocoons or dried Mayflies or other insects, also plentiful live insects, especially when the parents are feeding their young. These should be sprinkled with mineral substances. Bits of fruit and green food should be provided regularly and strawberries, blueberries, juniper berries and stewed fruits in winter are a welcome supplement.

The Shama should be kept in a heated room in winter.

DHYAL BIRD

(Copsychus saularis) Turdidae

The Dhyal Bird inhabits southeast Asia whence it has spread all the way to Bali. It frequents city parks and gardens in great numbers and also the vegetation on the margins of forests. The female is greyish-brown, the head and breast white with small brown spots. This bird is somewhat smaller than the Shama. Nesting takes place in a thicket or tree, sometimes also in holes in walls or in tree hollows. It is built of dry stalks and various fibres by the female. The female also hatches the four to five eggs, which she sits on for thirteen days while her mate feeds her. The newly hatched young are fed only by the hen at first but when they are older, also by the male. The birds are fledged at the age of twelve days and are fed by the parents for a further two to three weeks. At the age of five weeks they are able to fend for themselves.

In captivity, the female will gladly make use of an abandoned Blackbird's nest or a basket of rushes. A pair of these birds may be kept in a larger cage the same as for the Shama. The male is an excellent songster and sometimes even the female will try her hand at singing. The diet is the same as for the Shama but can be supplemented with small bits of cooked lean meat. The Dhyal Bird is also fond of fruits and soft berries. Stewed fruit may be provided in winter for variety. When the birds are feeding their young, the diet should include plenty of insects, e. g. mealworms, crickets, and also cockroaches. Earthworms, of which the adult birds are very fond, may be given on occasion.

This bird also requires a moist atmosphere, and specimens kept in an outdoor aviary should be taken into a heated room for the winter. If kept singly, this bird soon becomes tame and can be let out of its cage to fly about the room.

BLUE OR RED-BELLIED ROCK THRUSH

(Monticola solitarius) Turdidae

This bird makes its home chiefly in southern Europe, but is also found in Asia. It inhabits mainly coastal regions and occasionally occurs in central Europe, its favourite habitat being rocky sites, abandoned quarries and the like. The total length is about 28 cm (11 in). The female is greyish-brown with pale brown underparts and covered with spots shaped like half-moons. The young are like the hen in colouring. The nest is usually in a rock hollow, between stones or in a crevice in a quarry wall. The hen lays four to six bluish-green eggs, which she sits on for thirteen to fourteen days. After hatching, the parents take turns feeding the young. In the wild state, they feed primarily on insects and their larvae.

The Blue Rock Thrush is popular with aviculturists because of the male's lovely song. The cage should be roomy, however. A pair is better kept in an aviary, an outdoor one in summer, where the bird-keeper can build a rock garden to make the thrush feel at home. This species breeds only rarely in captivity.

Captive birds require plenty of insects in their diet, especially when feeding the young. Mealworms are recommended, sprinkled with mineral substances, crickets and ant cocoons and for variety an occasional locust, spider, hairless caterpillar and the like that can be obtained by sweeping. Also suitable are the caterpillars of the silkworm. Adult birds should furthermore be provided with a 'Thrush' mixture with egg, carrot, dried ant cocoons or Mayflies or other insects and may also be given cooked, ground, lean meat and in the autumn a few soft berries.

The Blue Rock Thrush should be taken indoors and kept in a heated room for the winter.

MOCKINGBIRD

(Mimus polyglottos) Mimidae

The Mockingbird inhabits the United States, Mexico and the West Indies. The female resembles the male but the colouring is not as bright. The total length is about 24 cm (9½ in). The nest of stalks, leaves, moss, wool, horsehair and bits of paper is built in thickets at a height of 1—2 m (40—80 in) or in a tree. The hen usually lays three to four eggs and sits on them for twelve to thirteen days. During this period she is fed by the male, who also assists in rearing the young, even though most of the care falls to the hen.

The male of this species is an extremely popular cage bird because of its lovely song which can be heard for more than half the year. Newly imported birds are sensitive to cold and should be protected, mainly against draughts. They are much hardier, however, after moulting and, having become acclimatized,can be put in an outdoor aviary for the summer. They can also be kept in the home in a larger cage with enough room for them to get ample exercise. These birds are avid eaters and the food dish must be constantly replenished. Lack of enough exercise causes them to get fat very quickly, whereupon they die shortly after. When feeding them mealworms there is a risk that the birds will become so used to them that they will refuse other food. Therefore it is better to give them insects captured by sweeping and a 'Nightingale' or 'Thrush' mixture. Soft berries may be given as a supplement.

Fledglings should be taken from the parents as soon as possible, about fourteen days after they leave the nest, for the older birds immediately begin to prepare to raise a new brood and the male attacks the young. A pair will sometimes breed up to three times in a year. Young males soon learn to sing very nicely.

HILL MYNAH

(Gracula religiosa) Sturnidae

The Hill Mynah is widespread in the northern parts of India, southern China and Hainan, and is also found in the Philippines. The sexes are alike in plumage and the length is 30 cm (12 in). The bird builds its nest in the hollows of trees where it also spends the night. The diet consists of insects and other invertebrates, fruits, berries and green shoots.

The Hill Mynah is very popular because of its excellent ability to mimic the human voice. It mimics words and even whole sentences so well that one would not believe they were being uttered by a bird. It also imitates the songs of various other birds, animal sounds, etc. In its native land it is called the 'Beo'. A robust bird, it requires a larger cage, at least 80 cm (32 in) long with the floor covered with a sheet of strong paper, which should be replaced by a clean sheet every day. Mynahs need an abundance of light and therefore the cage should be placed so that at least part is exposed to direct sunlight. The Hill Mynah rarely breeds in captivity.

It is an avid eater and care must be taken that it does not get fat by letting it out of the cage to fly about the room regularly after it has become tame, and by placing it in an outdoor aviary in the summer months where it has greater freedom of movement.

Newly imported birds should be fed a 'Thrush' mixture, also hardboiled egg, pieces of cooked meat, various insects, etc. Soft fruit should likewise be a regular part of the diet and berries, boiled rice, as well as green food such as spinach and lettuce, and stewed fruit in winter provide welcome variety.

ROSY PASTOR

(Sturnus roseus) Sturnidae

This species is widespread in Central Asia and Asia Minor, and likewise in southeastern Europe, finding its way on occasion even into central Europe. It winters in India. The sexes are alike in plumage and the total length is 23 cm (9 in). The young birds are coloured brownish-grey with spotted breasts. The nest of blades of dry grass, roots, wool, etc., is built in the hollows of trees and rocks and also on human dwellings. The clutch consists of four to six pale blue eggs which the parents take turns incubating for fourteen to fifteen days; both parents likewise share in feeding the young. The nestlings are fledged at the age of about three weeks, but are continually hungry and the parent birds are kept busy rearing their offspring. Out of the breeding season the Rosy Pastor congregates in large flocks which roam the countryside. It feeds chiefly on insects, mainly locusts, which it finds on the ground, though it also catches flying insects. Large colonies are often found in locations where there is an abundance of locusts. The birds also feed on beetles, spiders, snails and sometimes seeds, as well as the green parts of plants. On occasion they will eat various fruits and berries.

A captive pair requires a cage about 80 cm (32 in) long, 40 cm (16 in) wide and 60 cm (24 in) high. It breeds only rarely in confinement, and only in a roomier aviary provided with the usual nesting box. The diet consists of a 'Thrush' mixture, with an added supplement of various kinds of fruit and green food, such as spinach, lettuce, an insect or two and smaller seeds.

The Rosy Pastor is not as amusing as its European counterpart, the Common Sparrow, and it also does not learn to mimic human sounds. In winter it should be kept in a heated room.

GREEN GLOSSY STARLING

(Lamprocolius chalybaeus) Sturnidae

The Green Glossy Starling, like others of its kind, has a high metallic gloss on its feathers and attains a length of 25 cm (10 in). The sexes are alike in plumage. The home of this bird is Sudan, Somaliland, northern Uganda and Kenya. Nesting takes place in a tree hollow and the nest is made of grass, hairs, feathers and the like. The hen lays two to four greenish-blue eggs that are sometimes spotted, and sits on them herself for thirteen days. The male, however, shares the duties of rearing the young. These leave the nest after twenty days but are fed by the parent birds for a further two weeks. Out of the breeding season, Green Glossy Starlings congregate in flocks and roam the countryside in search of food — various insects, seeds and berries.

In captivity, these birds should be kept one pair to a cage, preferably at least 1 m (40 in) long, 40 cm (16 in) wide and 60 cm (2 ft) high. This species breeds frequently in confinement, but for this an aviary is more suitable and one provided with a nesting box somewhat smaller than for the Common Starling. After the young have become fledged, they should be removed from the parent birds so the latter can nest again. Suitable nesting material such as dry grass, moss, hairs, etc., should be placed in the aviary so the pair can line the nest themselves.

The diet consists of a 'Thrush' mixture, pieces of cooked lean meat, lettuce and other green food, various berries and an occasional insect or earthworm. When the young are being fed, insect food should be given daily, sprinkled with mineral substances, so that the young do not get rickets. Insects captured with a sweep net are good for this purpose. The birds may occasionally be given a little diluted syrup or water, sweetened with honey, to drink.

CRESTED MYNAH

(Acridotheres cristatellus) Sturnidae

The Crested Mynah, measuring 25—28 cm (10—11 in), is widespread in central and southern China and Vietnam. The female is the same as the male but has a smaller crest. During the breeding period the birds occur in pairs, but otherwise they gather in large flocks that roam the countryside. The nest is built in tree hollows, generally on the margins of tropical forests, near rivers, and sometimes even on tall buildings in cracks in the wall, e.g. in pagodas and the like. It seeks its food in open spaces and often raids rice fields during the harvest season. The hen lays two to five blue-green eggs and as a rule incubates them herself for thirteen to fourteen days. Both male and female, however, share in feeding the young. These leave the nest after nineteen to twenty days, but require parental care for about two more weeks.

Captive birds should be kept one pair to a larger cage, but nesting is more likely to occur in an aviary which is provided with a nesting box about the size of a starling's, though it may be larger — mynahs are not choosy. In an aviary Crested Mynahs may be kept together with smaller species of parrots or other birds of the same size, and even smaller species of pheasants.

The diet consists of a 'Thrush' mixture, fruit, various berries and also seeds. The birds should be given a regular supplement of green food such as spinach, lettuce and the like and some live insects now and then. When the young are being fed the insects should be sprinkled with mineral substances and given daily.

Crested Mynahs should be taken indoors and kept at room temperature for the winter. They are not difficult birds and given simple fare will live a long time in captivity.

ORIENTAL WHITE-EYE

(Zosterops palpebrosa) Zosteropidae

This small bird, only 10 cm (4 in) long, inhabits the woods and gardens of India and Ceylon and is also found as far away as the Philippines. It frequents the tree tops and bushes, where it flits about in search of small insects. It also feeds on the nectar from flowers and the sweet juice of ripe fruit. The beautifully constructed nest, a sort of ball made of fine grass, spiders' webs and small green leaflets, is hung among twigs. The clutch comprises two to four pale blue or green-blue eggs and the young hatch after eleven days.

In captivity this bird should be kept in a larger cage, for it is very active and constantly on the move. The cage may be provided with green plants, tall grass and the like. The Oriental White-eye breeds in confinement, but it is not an easy task to find a true pair, for the sexes are identical in plumage. The male, however, can be distinguished by his melodious song. The birds build their nest in a small basket which the aviculturist should place in dense greenery, and for this purpose should also provide nesting material such as fine coconut fibres, spiders' webs and fine grass.

The diet consists of a fine grade of 'Nightingale' mixture plus egg and ant cocoons or dried Mayflies, also small insects and, best of all, an assortment, obtained by sweeping, which should include spiders. Only the smallest of mealworms should be fed to these birds. Fresh fruit such as an orange cut in half crosswise, a halved pear or a wedge of banana should be a regular part of the diet, stewed fruit being a good substitute in the winter months. The liquid food should be a nectar of fruit juices, milk and honey.

SCARLET-BACKED FLOWERPECKER

(Dicaeum cruentatum) Dicaeidae

This species is a member of a very large group of small, usually brightly coloured birds which are widespread from northern India to southeast Asia and as far as the Moluccas and Sumatra. The female is olive-grey on the back with the rump and upper wing coverts scarlet. Another distinguishing feature of this species is their ragged tongue. The Scarlet-backed Flowerpecker frequents thickets or the tops of trees on the edges of tropical forests; however, it is also often found in gardens. It frequently visits flowering shrubs where it sucks the sweet nectar from the flowers with its specially adapted tongue. It is a very active bird, hopping and flitting from one twig to another in search of small insects, of which it is also fond. The nicely constructed sack-like nest with a narrow entrance hole in the upper part is built in tall bushes or trees.

Because it is so active, this bird requires a larger cage provided with twigs, although it is small in size. It is sensitive to cold and should therefore be kept in a heated room and best of all with a mate. However, it breeds very rarely in confinement.

The diet should include plenty of insects, best of all ones captured with a sweep net outdoors. In winter it should be given small crickets and the like. It should also be given juicy fruit, e. g. an orange cut in half, and in winter tinned peach halves, etc. A nectar food of juices plus condensed milk and honey is a welcome supplement. A fine-grade 'Nightingale' mixture with egg, carrot and ant cocoons or dried Mayflies or other insects may be given for variety now and then.

RED-LEGGED HONEYCREEPER

(Cyanerpes cyaneus) Coerebidae

This species is distributed throughout tropical America, from Mexico to southern Brazil and Bolivia, and is also plentiful in Cuba. A small bird, attaining a length of 12 cm (5 in), it is found in thin forests or in tree-tops along forest margins, whence it also ventures into parks and gardens. It often occurs in the company of tanagers. The female is dark green above, yellowish-green on the underparts and has brown legs. The male's winter garb resembles that of his mate but the legs are red. In the wild state, it feeds on nectar from flowers and small insects and their larvae.

In captivity, it may be kept in a larger cage, so that it has room to move around, or in an aviary together with tanagers. The diet of condensed milk with fruit juice and honey should be served in small, narrow dishes so that the birds do not soil their feathers. Also suitable is a container covered with wire netting, through which the Red-legged Honeycreeper can conveniently drink and on which it can even stand. Diluted syrups, an orange cut in half crosswise, a ripe banana and stewed fruit in the winter months may also be given. Likewise recommended is a fine-grade 'Nightingale' mixture and small insects, captured by sweeping, should be supplied twice a week.

The Red-legged Honeycreeper does not breed in captivity, but is one of the loveliest of the cage birds. During the summer it may be kept in an outdoor aviary, planted with several ornamental shrubs. In winter, however, it should be taken indoors. The twigs provided as perches should be replaced frequently, for they become sticky as the birds wipe their beaks on them and thus run the risk of unnecessarily soiling their feet and feathers.

MAGNOLIA WARBLER

(Dendroica magnolia) Parulidae

This small, 12 cm (5 in) bird is widespread in the eastern parts of North America. In winter it migrates to the Bahamas, Cuba, Haiti and even as far as Mexico and Panama. It frequents woods, parks and even gardens in large cities. The female is coloured grey instead of black and her other colours are not as bright as the male's. The young birds are olive-green above and yellowish on the underparts. The nest of fine bast, small twigs, various fibres, stalks and bark is lined with fine feathers and built high up in thickets and trees, usually between the two upright arms of a forked branch. The clutch consists of three to five white, brown-speckled eggs. In spring, when it arrives from its winter quarters, it frequents the vicinity of streams or rivers, whereas in the autumn, before its migratory flight, it is to be found in oak and birch woods. This species is the most numerous of the warblers. It is interesting to note that the song of the male shows great variety and that each cock has his own special song.

Magnolia Warblers may be kept in a cage in the home. They are extremely active birds and keep constantly on the move, even in confinement. Feeding is not difficult. The diet consists of the 'Nightingale' mixture with egg, grated carrot and ant cocoons or dried Mayflies, plus a regular ration of various kinds of insects, in summer ones that are caught outdoors by sweeping and, in winter, small mealworms or grubs. However, they are also fond of soft fruits which should be cut in half, e.g. orange, banana, etc., and in winter also some stewed fruit.

BOBOLINK

(Dolichonyx oryzivorus) Icteridae

The Bobolink makes its home in the eastern and central parts of the United States and southern Canada, spending the winter on the coast of Central America and in the West Indies. The bird measures 17.5 cm (7 in) and the winter plumage is the same for both sexes — yellowish-olive above, black wing tips, a red and yellow streak on the head, the underparts yellowish, the sides and back striped black-brown. The Bobolink gathers in large flocks on moist open spaces, often visiting rice, maize or other grain fields, where it is looked upon as an unwelcome guest. The nest of dry leaves, blades of grass, etc., lined with fine grass, is built in a hollow in the ground, usually in a meadow. Four to seven pale brown eggs, covered with grey and rufous streaks and blotches, form the clutch. The young hatch in thirteen to fourteen days and take about the same time to become fledged.

A pair of these birds may be kept in a roomy cage or several pairs in an aviary, where they sometimes breed. An aviary may also contain other species of birds of the same size.

During the breeding season, it feeds mainly on insects, which it also gives to its offspring. Later, the diet includes various seeds, grain, the green parts of plants, etc. In captivity the diet should consist of millet, canary seed, and unripe ears of oats on occasion. Wetted grain seeds may also be given as may the 'Thrush' mixture and live insects throughout the year. Unfortunately, the male often loses its handsome plumage in confinement.

RED-WINGED BLACKBIRD

(Agelaius humeralis) Icteridae

This member of the genus *Agelaius* inhabits the Greater Antilles, chiefly Cuba, where it is one of the commonest birds. It measures 17.5 cm (7 in) and the only difference between the male and female is that the latter has a smaller, red-brown patch on the wing. The nest, woven of stalks, plant fibres, etc., and lined with fine hairs and feathers, is built in thick reeds. The clutch comprises four to five pale blue, brown-spotted eggs and the young hatch after thirteen to fourteen days. In the wild state, it feeds on seeds which it finds in fields, and during the breeding season chiefly on insects, larvae, spiders and small molluscs.

A pair of Red-winged Blackbirds may be kept in a larger cage and several specimens in an aviary, which may also contain other species of birds of the same size. It breeds in confinement and should therefore be provided with a partially lined, deep basket which it finishes by itself from material the aviculturist should remember to provide, i. e. grass and the like. During the nesting period, the diet should include the 'Nightingale' mixture and live insects, e.g. mealworms and crickets. Otherwise, suitable foods are small seeds such as millet and canary seed. The Red-winged Blackbird is also fond of whole heads of plantain, unripe oats, etc., and an occasional supplement of green food — spinach, dandelion leaves, etc. — provides welcome variety.

This bird is very hardy and may be kept outdoors until late autumn, but should be taken inside and kept at room temperature for the winter.

SCARLET TANAGER

(Piranga olivacea) Thraupidae

The Scarlet Tanager inhabits southeastern Canada and the eastern United States, but winters in the West Indies or Central America. The female is olive-green which is lighter below, with a brownish-grey tail and wing feathers. The non-breeding plumage of the male is likewise olive-green, but the wing and tail feathers retain their black colour. The nest of roots, stalks, and pieces of bark is lined with fine bark and built on the horizontal branches of trees. The hen lays three to five

The diet consists of insects, soft fruit and berries, but the Scarlet

green-blue eggs covered with chestnut spots. As a rule the female incubates the eggs alone for thirteen days, the male taking a turn only rarely. However, both parents share in rearing the young.

Tanager is also fond of bees, ants and smaller beetles. In the woods it is adroit at finding caterpillars, and picking out those that are encased in thick cocoons. It also eats butterfly eggs and on occasion, small seeds.

In captivity, a pair may be kept in a roomy cage or aviary; in the latter, these birds tolerate other tanagers or various other smaller species of birds as companions.

The basic diet consists of fresh soft fruit such as oranges, bananas, soft pears and, in winter, stewed fruit. Mealworms, grasshoppers or other insects should be supplied regularly. Also welcomed now and then is a bee larva — the tanagers remove them from the honeycomb themselves. Recommended liquid foods are diluted juices with honey and the like. In winter, even a few small seeds such as millet and canary seed may be included in the diet.

STRIPE-HEADED TANAGER

(Spindalis zena) Thraupidae

This tanager makes its home in Cuba and the neighbouring Isle of Pines. It measures about 13 cm (5 in). The female has olive-green underparts, grey streaks on the head, olive breast, grey flanks and brown-black wing and tail feathers edged with olive. The young resemble the hen except that the young males are more olive-green above. During the breeding season the birds live in pairs, but otherwise they gather in small flocks. They frequently invade orange plantations where they eat the soft flesh of the fruit. They also eat large numbers of insects and their larvae.

In captivity, a pair may be kept in a larger cage, in summer in an outdoor aviary, which may also contain other tolerant birds of like size. However they must be taken indoors into a heated room for the winter.

The diet comprises various fruits, e.g. an orange cut in half, a piece of banana, ripe pear, peach, etc., and, in winter, stewed fruit. The Stripe-headed Tanager will also accept an egg mixture with carrot and ant cocoons or dried Mayflies or other insects. Live insects as well as some small seeds such as millet, canary seed, etc., provide welcome variety.

Stripe-headed Tanagers enjoy bathing and should, therefore, be provided with a shallow dish filled with water for this purpose. Twiggy branches in the cage should be washed regularly or replaced by new ones, for they become very soiled and sticky from the fruit juices that the birds rub off their beaks. The Stripe-headed Tanager has not as yet been known to breed in captivity.

CARDINAL OR VIRGINIAN CARDINAL

(Pyrrhuloxia cardinalis) Fringillidae

This bird, measuring 19—22 cm (7 ½—8 ½ in), inhabits eastern North America. The female is predominantly yellow-brown with a dark red crest. The Cardinal is found in cultivated lands where it eats various insect pests in the fields, and also the seeds of various weeds, and is therefore man's great ally. The nest is built of twigs, stalks, moss and fibres within two to three days. The clutch comprises three to five spotted eggs varying in colour. They are incubated by the hen alone for twelve to fourteen days. During this time she is provided with food by the male, who now and then loudly sings his song from some higher perch. The young grow very rapidly and often leave the nest after nine days, though they are not able to fend for themselves until after four weeks.

A pleasant cage bird, the Cardinal rapidly becomes tame if kept singly. The male's plumage fades after a time though this may be avoided if the bird is fed live insects, carrot juice, Rowan berries, and the like. Otherwise, the diet may include just millet, oats, wheat and the like, plus plenty of green food. Blueberries, a ripe tomato, a piece of apple and diluted fruit juices provide welcome variety. In winter the bird may be given the twigs of fruit trees with buds. When the young are being fed, insects and a 'Thrush' mixture are a must, the latter, of course, may be fed to adult specimens throughout the year.

During the breeding season, Cardinals should be kept in pairs; otherwise they tolerate other, even smaller, birds.

RED-CRESTED CARDINAL

(Paroaria coronata) **Fringillidae**

This cardinal measuring 19 cm (7½ in), inhabits the southeastern parts of South America, where it occurs in forest margins as well as in parks. The nest of twigs, stalks, moss and the like is built by both the male and female in dense evergreens. The hen lays two to five eggs which she mostly incubates alone for twelve to fourteen days in the wild, and in captivity as much as sixteen days. The young are fledged after fourteen to seventeen days, but continue to be fed for another two weeks by the male while the hen prepares to raise another brood.

The Red-crested Cardinal is a very active bird in confinement and should be kept singly or in pairs in a larger cage about 80 cm (32 in) long, 50 cm (20 in) wide and 60 cm (24 in) high. A pair should have the cage to themselves, but in an aviary they may have other birds as companions. A hardy bird, it can be left in an outdoor aviary from spring until late autumn. Some aviculturists in coastal regions leave it there throughout the winter, although this is not recommended. It breeds well in captivity in an aviary, less frequently in a large cage. An abandoned Blackbird's nest may be provided for this purpose or else a basket of reeds, which it then completes itself.

An aviary should be planted with evergreens, for instance junipers, where the Red-crested Cardinal likes to build its nest.

The diet in confinement consists of small seeds such as millet, canary seed, unhulled rice, plus a plentiful supply of fruits and green food and, on occasion, twiggy branches with young shoots. The 'Thrush' mixture is also suitable. When the young are being fed, the diet should include insects, egg mixture and fresh ant cocoons. In winter, it will appreciate pieces of stewed fruit.

PAINTED BUNTING OR NONPAREIL

(Passerina ciris) Fringillidae

This bunting makes its home in the southeastern United States, the Bahamas and Cuba, where it frequents the outskirts of woods and gardens. The total length is 12.5—14 cm (5—5 ½ in) and the female, as well as the young, is greenish with olive-brown flanks. The nest is built of small twigs, roots and grass blades in low thickets or in the thick foliage of young trees, by the female alone. The clutch consists of four to five pale blue eggs with red-brown spots. The female alone incubates them for about thirteen days and the young are fledged at the age of eleven to twelve days. The male keeps careful guard over the nest with the young and even helps to feed them, but the chief responsibility is the hen's. In confinement, the male does not feed the nestlings at all, as a rule.

The Painted Bunting is a popular cage bird and was already being kept as a pet in eighteenth-century London. A pair may be kept in a cage or aviary, where it also nests quite frequently. Out of the breeding season it gets along well with other birds but during the nesting period the male chases stronger birds from the vicinity of the nest. The aviculturist should provide the Painted Bunting with a thicket of reeds and twigs and either an old finch's nest or else a nesting box or semi-box. Some pairs raise as many as three broods in a year.

The Painted Bunting is an easy bird to feed and will live on millet and canary seed, plus an occasional ration of 'Nightingale' egg mixture with ant cocoons and ground cooked meat. It is fond of a mealworm, crickets or other insects now and then and these should be provided regularly when the young are being fed. Birds kept in cages tend to become overfat and the bright plumage of many males tends to fade after several moultings.

INDIGO BUNTING

(Passerina cyanea) Fringillidae

This bunting is widely distributed from eastern North America to Central America, the Bahamas and Cuba, where it frequents the outskirts of woods and also visits gardens. The total length is about 12.5 cm (5 in). The female, like the male in his winter garb, is coloured rufous-brown above, with a whitish throat and underparts. The nest is built by the female, the male bringing her various nesting materials such as stalks, twigs, and the like. Three to four pale blue eggs form the clutch, which is incubated for thirteen to fourteen days by the hen alone, the male providing her with food during this time. The young leave the nest at the age of twelve days or so. The natural diet consists of insects, green food and small seeds, the young being fed primarily insects and their larvae.

In confinement, a pair may be kept in a cage or aviary where they tolerate the company of other birds except during the nesting period, when they become aggressive and pluck the feathers of smaller species. An old finch nest or a basket of reeds provides a good framework for building their own nest.

The Indigo Bunting should be fed millet, canary seed and soaked seeds. It is also fond of fruit, spinach and dandelion leaves. The 'Nightingale' mixture may be given for variety and is a must when feeding the young, which should also be provided with insects.

This is a hardy bird and may be kept in an outdoor aviary till the end of October. In captivity the male tends to lose his bright colouring which becomes faded and dull. The Indigo Bunting can be successfully cross-bred with a Canary and they produce attractively coloured hybrids.

CUBAN FINCH

(Tiaris canora) Fringillidae

This small bird, measuring only 9.5 cm (4 in), inhabits the island of Cuba, where it is generally found in bushy sites with grass cover. The female has a grey-brown crown and the parts which are coloured black in the male are brown in the hen. The Cuban Finch feeds on grass seeds, insects and green leaflets. The dome-shaped nest is made of grass and moss and has a tunnel-like entrance. Both partners share the task of building, which takes four to six days. The hen lays three to four white to blue-green eggs which have black-brown spots. She alone incubates them for twelve, thirteen or even fifteen days. At the age of thirteen to sixteen days, the young leave the nest fully feathered, but are still fed by the male for a short time after. After twenty-four days the young birds are fully independent.

The Cuban Finch is very active in confinement, and a single pair should be kept in a cage by themselves, for the male is very quarrelsome towards other birds and often attacks them, this being so even in an aviary during the nesting period. In a larger cage it will build its nest in a nesting box.

The diet consists of small seeds such as millet, canary seed, various grass seeds and whole ears or heads of plantain, etc. It should include an abundance of green food such as spinach, lettuce, chickweed and grass. When rearing the young, the birds should be given a 'Nightingale' mixture and fresh ant cocoons, also small live insects and their larvae. 'Soft' food with egg and carrot may be given even to adult birds now and then. The Cuban Finch is very hardy and may be kept in a coldish room during the winter. It is possible to distinguish the male from the female by the age of nine to ten weeks.

CANARY

(Serinus canaria) Fringillidae

The Canary's original home is the Canary Islands, Madeira and the Azores, whence it was introduced into Europe in 1478 after the conquest of the Canary Islands by the Spaniards. In Spain, it was kept only by monks and in the mid-sixteenth century found its way from that country to Italy and thence to the Tyrol, where it was bred and became known throughout the world. Over the decades many colour varieties as well as many breeds differing in size and appearance (with crest, curly feathers, etc.) have been evolved by selective breeding.

Today there are countless clubs and societies made up of Canary-breeders, who organize exhibitions, provide information and advice to members, etc.

Canaries should be kept singly (the male) or in pairs. Some aviculturists provide a male with several mates. For breeding purposes the cage should be provided with a wire basket lined with felt, but a semi-nesting box will do just as well, the Canary lining it itself with various fibrous materials before nesting. The hen often begins sitting as soon as the first egg is laid and therefore this and ensuing eggs should be removed and replaced by artificial ones until the clutch is complete (four to six eggs), so that the young will hatch all at one time. The incubation period is thirteen days and the young leave the nest when about eighteen days old, being fed by the parents for one week more. The cage for breeding Canaries should be about 50 cm (20 in) long, 40 cm (16 in) wide and 40 cm (16 in) high.

The staple diet consists of seeds, sweet rape seed, canary seed, niger seed, poppyseed, lettuce seed, hulled oats, crushed hemp seed, also millet, sprays of grass, green food, a piece of apple now and then and for the young a 'Nightingale' mixture and a few insects. The Canary is fond of bathing.

RED-BILLED QUELEA

(Quelea quelea) Ploceidae

This bird inhabits the eastern parts of tropical Africa. The total length is about 11 cm (4 ½ in). The male when out of colour resembles the female, which is mainly grey-brown. During the breeding season the hen has a yellow beak, which later turns black, whereas the male's is permanently red. Nesting takes place in tree branches or bushes and also in tall grass. The nest is built chiefly by the male; he fashions several constructions from which the hen takes her choice and then helps to complete it. The clutch consists of three to seven eggs and the incubation period is fourteen days. The young are fed by both parents with grass and other seeds as well as insects and other invertebrates.

In captivity, several pairs kept together sometimes breed. However, one pair in a small cage will not. The cage for a single pair should be about 80 cm (32 in) long, 50 cm (20 in) wide and 60 cm (24 in) high, though it may be even larger. An aviary, however, is more suitable and may contain reeds, dry grass and the like for the Red-billed Queleas to build their nests in. These are constructed of fine grass, coconut fibres, bast, fine reed stalks, etc. An aviary may include other species of birds for this bird is amiable towards others.

If one wants the Red-billed Quelea to nest in confinement, the male and female must come from the same locality, for the various races have different nesting periods as well as different nesting biology, e. g. construction of the nest, and this plays an important role. A dealer will sometimes have several Red-billed Queleas from different areas of the birds' distribution and these individuals will never pair. During the winter months, the Red-billed Quelea should be kept in a heated room.

RED BISHOP

(Euplectes orix) Ploceidae

This bird occurs in several races throughout Africa, chiefly in Senegal, Cameroon, Uganda and the Upper Nile basin. The total length is 11—12 cm (4 ½ in). The eclipse plumage of both sexes is alike — pale brown above and whitish below. It inhabits grassland areas and feeds mainly on grass seeds and partly also on insects. The domed nest of long blades of grass, fibres, strips of bast, etc., is built on the twiggy branches of trees or in tall bushes. The hen lays two to four blue eggs and incubates them for about fourteen days. Care of the offspring is likewise mainly the task of the hen.

In captivity, a single pair may be kept in a cage or several pairs in an aviary together with other species of smaller birds. When out of colour these birds are amiable to others, but during the nesting period the males are aggressive and require more room, and defend their nesting territory. At this time they should be provided with long blades of grass, strips of bast, coconut fibres and the like with which to build the nest. For this purpose they also require a number of forked branches in the aviary. Though the Red Bishop may begin building a nest in captivity, it often leaves the construction unfinished and does not breed. Even so, the cleverly woven structure is a pretty sight.

The Red Bishop should be fed various seeds, such as millet and canary seed, with a supplement of a few mealworms or other insects and maybe egg mixture with carrot and a piece of fruit for variety. This bird is very easy to care for in confinement. In winter it should be kept in a heated room.

GRENADIER WEAVER

(Euplectes afra) Ploceidae

This species inhabits Africa south of the Sahara, but is most abundant in the territory stretching from Senegal to the Sudan, where it occurs in grasslands mainly in the vicinity of lakes and rivers. The total length is 10—11 cm (4—4 ½ in) and the eclipse plumage of the male resembles that of the female — dark brown above, whitish on the underparts and a yellow-brown stripe above the eye. The nest is built on the branches of trees or in tall thickets. It is a suspended construction of grass and bast fibres, which the birds peel from trees, and is mainly the male's concern. The female lays two to four white eggs, spotted grey and black, and she incubates them alone for fourteen days. The young are fledged at the age of three weeks or so. The hen will not take to every nest the male builds and if it is not to her liking will refuse it. The Grenadier Weaver feeds mainly on the seeds of grass and insects. Swarming termites attract whole flocks of these birds, who also feed them to their young. Flocks will also raid cultivated fields.

In captivity, Grenadier Weavers may be kept one pair to a cage, or several individuals in an aviary, which may also contain other weavers and other species of birds of about the same size. This weaver is easy to feed, the diet consisting of various seeds and green food and an occasional supplement of insects or egg mixture. During the nesting period it should be provided with grass, coconut fibres, the foliage of reeds, thin roots and the like as nesting material. This species also often leaves its nest unfinished in captivity. The Grenadier Weaver lives to a great age in confinement.

GOLDEN SPARROW

(Passer luteus) Ploceidae

This bird is a native of northeastern and central Africa, being particularly numerous in the Sudan. The total length is about 12.5 cm (5 in). The female is coloured yellow-brown above, whitish below, with black-brown flanks, wings and tail. It congregates in large flocks, often even during the nesting season, being a colonial breeder. The nest of fine grasses is built by the female in low trees. The clutch is three to four white to greenish eggs spotted grey-brown. They are incubated by the hen alone for eleven to thirteen days. The young leave the nest at the age of nine to fourteen days, but continue to be fed by the parents for several more days.

In confinement, it may be kept in a cage, which a pair has to itself, or in an aviary with other small birds which it tolerates. It breeds well in captivity, often even in cages. In this case, however, it prefers a wooden nesting box which the female lines with fine grass, hairs and feathers. It breeds very well in an aviary, especially an outdoor one, and many pairs will rear as many as three broods in a year. It is interesting to note that in confinement it rarely builds its own nest. The young are fed primarily by the female. In captivity it is easily cross-bred with the Common Sparrow.

The Golden Sparrow is an easy bird to feed. The diet consists of various seeds such as millet, canary seed, hemp, rape, etc. It may be given a spray of grass or plantain heads on occasion and a regular ration of green food such as chickweed, spinach, dandelion or lettuce. When rearing the young the birds should be given the 'Nightingale' mixture with egg daily for the first five to seven days and also plentiful insects. In winter, the Golden Sparrow should be kept in heated quarters.

QUEEN WHYDAH

(Vidua regia) Ploceidae

This species inhabits southern and southwest Africa, occurring in grassland areas. The total length is about 10 cm (4 in), but when in breeding plumage the male grows very long tail feathers. When out of colour the male greatly resembles the female, which is brownish with a black crown, whitish underparts, brown wings and tail, and a black stripe above the eye. This bird is a nesting parasite; the female lays her eggs in the nests of finches, usually that of the Violet-eared Waxbill *(Uraeginthus granatinus)*, always throwing out one of the host's eggs first.

Aviculturists should keep one pair to a cage measuring about 80 cm (32 in) in length, 50 cm (20 in) in width and 60 cm (24 in) in height, though an aviary is preferable, in which it may be kept with other birds as companions out of the breeding season of course. During the nesting period the males are very aggressive, and for this reason the pair should be provided with separate quarters; it is likewise impossible to keep two males together. Even if provided with the company of finches, it rarely breeds in captivity.

The diet consists of various seeds such as millet, canary, rape and niger, also sprays of grass, plantain heads and the like. Green food — chickweed, spinach, etc. — should be provided regularly. On occasion, especially during the courting period, when the birds moult, they may be given live insects or larvae, plus egg mixture. During the summer, the Queen Whydah may be kept in an outdoor aviary, but should be taken indoors for the winter and put in a heated room.

RED-CHEEKED CORDON BLEU

(Uraeginthus bengalensis) Estrildidae

This pretty bird inhabits the dry areas of Africa, south of the Sahara, occurring often in the vicinity of human habitations. The total length is 12 cm (5 in) and the sexes are very much alike, although the female lacks the crimson ear patch. The nest is of grass and feathers and is usually built by the female in a bush; often, however, also in a thatched roof or abandoned weaver's nest. The entrance hole is at the side. The clutch consists of four to seven white eggs. The young hatch in eleven to thirteen days and leave the nest, fully capable of flight, after fourteen days. In the wild state the Red-cheeked Cordon Bleu feeds on various seeds and also insects.

This bird may be kept one pair to a cage. However, it rarely breeds here and therefore it is better to house it in an aviary where it may have other small birds as companions. In confinement it builds its nest in a thicket, but also welcomes a semi-nesting box. It is very shy and timid during the nesting season and requires the maximum of privacy, often abandoning the nest if disturbed.

Newly imported birds are delicate and should be kept in warmer quarters with the temperature at about 22 °C. They soon become acclimatized, however, and can then be kept even in outdoor aviaries.

The diet consists of canary seed, millet, flax, rape and niger seed, and various seeding grasses, also a regular ration of chickweed, spinach, or a bit of lettuce. When rearing their young, the birds should be given egg food, e.g. the 'Nightingale' mixture, and live insects or larvae. Live insects may also be given to adult birds on occasion.

RED AVADAVAT

(Estrilda amandava) Estrildidae

This bird is widely distributed in India and southeastern Asia. The length is 9—10 cm (3½—4 in), and the eclipse plumage of the male resembles that of the female, which is brownish with a yellow-red rump and throat and yellow-white underparts and wing coverts, spotted with tiny white spots. The Red Avadavat is found in forest margins or bushes in open grassland areas. The domed nest with the entrance at the side is made of grass and lined with feathers and small leaflets. It is built in a bush or tree, chiefly by the male. The hen lays four to six white eggs. The young hatch after twelve to thirteen days and are fledged at the age of sixteen days.

In captivity, the Red Avadavat can be kept one pair to a cage, or several pairs in an aviary together with other smaller birds. It breeds well in an aviary but requires plentiful thickets, reeds, grass and the like.

The Red Avadavat is easy to feed. The diet consists of various small seeds and a regular supplement of green food. When rearing the young, the birds should also be given an egg mixture, e.g. the 'Nightingale' mixture, plus some small insects or fresh ant cocoons.

Sometimes dealers sell 'green' Avadavats which, however, lose this colour after the first moult and turn red (males). This custom of dyeing the bird's feathers is particularly widespread in the East where the price asked for the bird is then higher. The true Green Avadavat *(Estrilda formosa)* is a native of central India. In the winter months, Red Avadavats should be kept in heated quarters.

BENGALESE FINCH

(Lonchura striata f. domestica) Estrildidae

The Bengalese Finch is actually a domesticated bird reared in captivity in Japan and China many, many years ago. The bird as it is known in its present form in captivity does not occur in the wild. It is believed to have been bred from the White-backed Munia or Striated Finch *(Lonchura striata)*. Bengalese Finches occur in various colour forms, e.g. pure white, brown, yellow-brown, as well as striped. The male resembles the female and can be definitely distinguished only by his song.

Bengalese Finches may be kept in confinement in a cage about 50 cm (20 in) long, 40 cm (16 in) wide and 50 cm (20 in) high, which a pair should have to themselves. An aviary may contain several pairs along with other birds of the same size. If one wants the birds to nest, they should be provided with a box or semi-box 12 cm (5 in) square and 15 cm (6 in) high, plus fine dry grass, wool and mixed fibres with which to line the nest. The clutch consists of five eggs. The young hatch after fourteen days and leave the nest three weeks later, though they continue to be fed by the parents for a further two weeks. The aviculturist who has a pair in a cage should remove the young so that the parent birds may start another brood. The diet consists of the 'Nightingale' mixture, small insects, small germinating seeds, green food such as chickweed and spinach. Adult birds should be fed chiefly seeds, e.g. millet or canary, and a regular ration of green food and egg mixture on occasion for variety.

The Bengalese Finch willingly incubates the eggs of other birds and will rear the young perfectly when they hatch. Advantage is often taken of this characteristic by putting the eggs of rarer birds who refuse to incubate in captivity under the Bengalese Finch to hatch.

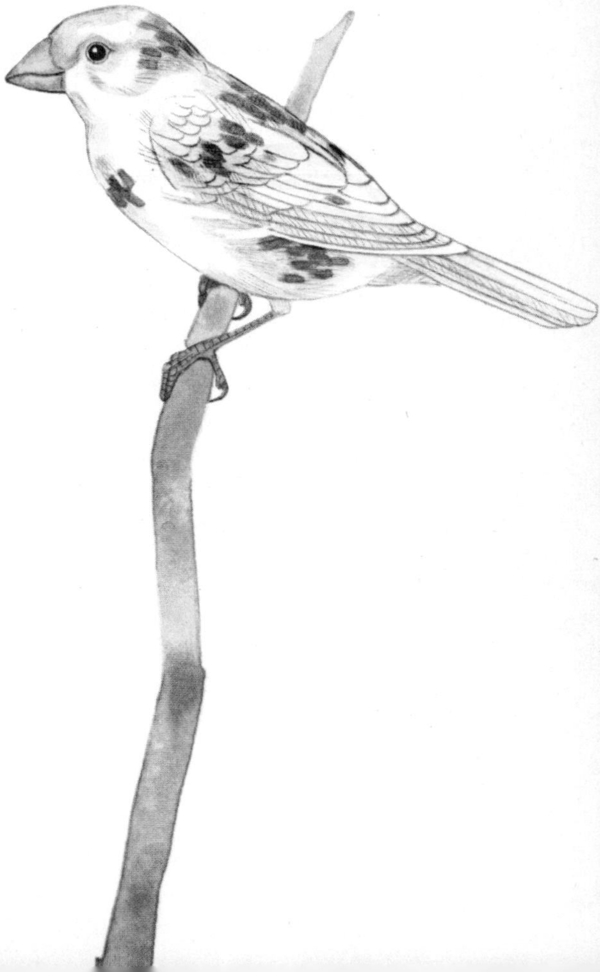

THREE-COLOURED MUNIA

(Lonchura malacca malacca) Estrildidae

This species inhabits India and Ceylon, where it gathers in small flocks usually in the vicinity of water. It also invades neighbouring rice fields. The total length is about 11.5 cm ($4\frac{1}{2}$ in) and the sexes are alike. The nest is of dry grass, bast, and the like and is located in bamboo thickets or reeds. The clutch consists of four to six white eggs and the incubating period is eleven to thirteen days. The young leave the nest at the age of sixteen to eighteen days. In the wild it feeds on seeds of various grasses, rice, which it takes in the unripe state, green leaves and occasionally, when rearing young, also insects.

The Three-coloured Munia may be kept in a cage, which a pair has to themselves, or in an aviary together with other birds of the same size as companions, for these Munias are very amiable. In captivity it will breed in a cage. For this purpose it should be provided with a small basket or semi-nesting box and fine dry grass, hairs, coconut fibres, etc., with which to line the nest. In the case of a larger cage or aviary, part of it may consist of a reed 'jungle' containing an abandoned bird's nest which it will adopt as its own.

The diet in confinement consists of various small seeds such as millet and canary, some green food and, especially when rearing the young, a supplement of 'Nightingale' mixture with egg, carrot and ant cocoons.

The Black-headed Munia *(Lonchura malacca atricapilla)* is a subspecies and has the entire head and throat a glossy black. The female of this form also resembles the male. It inhabits northern India, whence it has spread as far as southern Burma.

SILVERBILL

(Lonchura malabarica) Estrildidae

This bird has two races — the Indian Silverbill *(Lonchura malabarica malabarica)* which inhabits India and Ceylon and the African Silverbill *(L. m. cantans)* of Africa. The Indian form has the tail coverts white, whereas those of its African counterpart are black. The sexes are alike in plumage and the total length is 11 cm (4 ½ in). When out of colour, the birds congregate in small flocks in open country with bushes, and also in plantations and gardens. The nest is built in a bush or the branches of a tree, often between the sticks supporting eagles' nests, and in the case of the African Silverbill even in the nests of weavers. It is composed of grasses and other materials. One nest may often contain more than twenty white eggs laid by several hens. The young hatch after twelve to fourteen days. The diet in the wild state consists of seeds of grasses, green leaves and partly also insects.

In captivity it breeds well, even in a cage. The Indian Silverbill, however, is better at rearing the young. In an aviary it will build its nest of grass in the branches of thickets, but will also avail itself of a box or semi-nesting box lined with wool and feathers. The nesting boxes should be attached to the cage from the outside so as not to take up unnecessary space.

Silverbills are very easy to care for. They should be fed various small seeds such as millet, canary and grass seeds, unripe sprays of grass and a regular ration of green food such as chickweed, plus a few insects for variety. When rearing the young the diet should consist of an egg mixture, say the 'Nightingale' mixture, and a plentiful supply of insects. In a larger cage or aviary Silverbills may be kept together with other species of birds for they are quite amiable. Some pairs will even rear the young of other species.

ZEBRA FINCH

(Poephila guttata) Estrildidae

The Zebra Finch is widespread in Australia, where it inhabits grasslands and bushy localities. The female differs from the male in that she lacks the chestnut ear patch and the barring. Captive birds include various colour forms, e.g. white, yellow-brown and the like.

The nest is constructed of dry grass and feathers. The clutch comprises four to seven white eggs which both parents take turns incubating for eleven to twelve days. The young are fledged at the age of three weeks. The diet in the wild state consists chiefly of the seeds of various grasses.

The Zebra Finch is an ideal cage bird for beginners as it breeds extremely well. A pair may be kept in a cage or several individuals in an aviary together with other smaller birds as companions. The Zebra Finch nests at any time of the year but the hen may become egg-bound in cold weather. For this reason, if kept outdoors, the birds should be taken inside by September and installed in heated quarters. A small wooden nesting box, shallow basket, an old nest of some other bird or even a box made of hard paper may be provided for nesting purposes. The Zebra Finch will then line it itself with fine dry grass, moss, various fibres, feathers, etc.

The Zebra Finch should be fed small seeds such as millet, canary or rape, sprays of grass and also green food — chickweed, spinach, a bit of lettuce and the like. Just before the breeding season a Cuttlefish bone may be hung in the cage. When rearing their young, the birds should be given a 'Nightingale' egg mixture and some live insects now and then. Young birds are capable of breeding at the age of three months but it is better to wait till the following year.

JAVA SPARROW

(Padda oryzivora) Estrildidae

The Java Sparrow, a somewhat heavily built bird with a large beak, was originally a native of Java and the island of Bali whence it was introduced by man to other islands and is now widespread not only in southeastern Asia but also in eastern Africa and Zanzibar. It is also called the Rice-bird, for rice is its favourite food, and it also feeds on other seeds including cultivated grains. A white form that is practically a domesticated bird has been bred in Japan: it breeds more freely in captivity than the wild form.

The Java Sparrow builds its dome-shaped nest of grass in the branches of trees, as well as in tree hollows and underneath the roofs of houses. It is a colonial nester. The clutch consists of four to seven white eggs and the incubation period is twelve to fourteen days. The young leave the nest at the age of four weeks but continue to be fed by the parents a short while longer.

Newly imported birds will often not begin to breed until after three or four years. A pair should be kept in a cage about 1 m (40 in) long, 50 cm (20 in) wide and 70 cm (28 in) high. Single specimens may be kept in a smaller cage. For nesting they should be provided with a semi-nesting box 16 cm (6 in) square and 20 cm (8 in) high, with fine feathers, dry grass, etc., as nesting material.

The diet consists of millet, canary seed, rape, hemp, oats, wheat, unhulled rice, ears of grain, etc., plus plenty of green food, and prior to the breeding period crushed egg shells. The young should be fed a 'Nightingale' mixture and a few mealworms daily. The Java Sparrow is fond of bathing and will welcome a shallow dish with water. In an aviary, it may be kept together with other birds, even smaller species.

STAR FINCH OR RUFICAUDA

(Bathilda ruficauda) Estrildidae

This bird is widespread in Australia, where it occurs in five races. The sexes are alike in plumage, but the female is duller and has less red on the head. The total length is 11 cm (4½ in). It is usually found in open, grassy spaces in the vicinity of water and wherever there are reeds and bushes. The nest of grass is globular with a tunnel-like entrance and is built in bushes or in low trees. The hen lays three to five white eggs and the young hatch eleven to thirteen days later. The diet consists chiefly of various grass and other seeds and to a lesser degree of insects and spiders.

In captivity it may be kept in a cage (one pair) or in an aviary in the company of other small birds with which it gets on well. In confinement it is more likely to breed in an aviary supplied with reeds and thickets and perhaps a shallow bath. Grass, wool, horsehair and the like should be provided for nesting purposes. It rarely breeds in a cage.

The Star Finch soon becomes acclimatized and is then very hardy, and many individuals live to a great age. It may be put in an outdoor aviary with the arrival of spring, but should be kept in heated quarters during the winter.

The recommended diet is millet, canary seed, rape seed, flax, niger seed and the seeds of various grasses, even unripe sprays and plantain heads. Green food such as chickweed, spinach, dandelion, lettuce and grass should be provided regularly. When rearing the young, the diet should be supplemented with a 'Nightingale' egg mixture and a daily ration of insects or larvae. Also suitable are insects obtained by sweeping or small spiders.

BLUE-FACED PARROT FINCH

(Erythrura trichroa) Estrildidae

This bird occurs in several races in northern Australia, New Guinea, the Moluccas, Caroline and neighbouring islands. The female and male have similar plumage but the hen is duller. The total length is 12—13 cm (5 in). Favouring areas where there are bushes, it builds its nest of various plant fibres in their branches. The three to six white eggs that form the clutch are hatched after thirteen to fourteen days.

The Blue-faced Parrot Finch is best kept in a larger cage for it is very active. An amiable and peaceable species, it may also be kept in an aviary with other birds. In either case it should be provided with a thicket of reeds which it likes to climb in and out of. Newly imported specimens usually do not breed for several years in captivity, and the aviculturist should therefore not be put off by initial failures. When he has finally succeeded in getting the birds to nest, the young should be removed when they have become fledged, for they are sometimes attacked by the male. There is no such danger in an aviary with ample space.

The birds should be fed small seeds such as white and Indian millet, canary, hemp, hulled oats and rape seed. Green food such as blades of grass, some spinach, dandelion and chickweed should be a regular supplement. Occasionally insects, mealworms, crickets or insects obtained by sweeping, provide welcome variety. Live insects, of course, are a must when rearing young and also a 'Nightingale' egg mixture.

GOULDIAN FINCH

(Poephila gouldiae) Estrildidae

This bird inhabits northern Australia where it occurs in two varieties — the Red-headed and Black-headed. In captivity one also comes across Yellow-headed specimens. The sexes are alike in plumage, but the hen is duller. The total length is 13 cm (5 in). This finch frequents open grassy spaces in the vicinity of water. The nest of grass is built in a bush, clumps of tall grass or even in the hollow branch of a tree. The hen lays four to eight white eggs which she and the male take turns incubating for thirteen to fourteen days. Young nestlings have a cluster of phosphorescent nodules at the base of the beak which aid the parents in placing the food in the darkness of the nest. The chief food is grass seeds.

The Gouldian Finch may be kept one pair to a cage measuring 80 cm (32 in) in length, 60 cm (24 in) in width and 60 cm (24 in) in height. Several pairs may be kept in an aviary together with other birds. A small nesting box and nesting materials such as dry grass, fibres, etc., should be provided during the breeding season. When rearing the young a 'Nightingale' mixture and small insects should be provided for the first few days, various seeds such as millet and canary being fed them from the fourth day on. Other suitable seeds are rape, niger, flax, poppy, lettuce, and sprays of grass. Green food should also be supplied. Some aviculturists recommend giving the birds a piece of charred wood, as in the wild state they are often found in burned-out spaces. Nesting birds may also be given a piece of egg before the young hatch.

The Gouldian Finch is more difficult to care for. It requires a temperature of about 20 °C when nesting and does not tolerate cold weather.

CUT-THROAT MANNIKIN

(Amadina fasciata) Estrildidae

This bird inhabits Africa from Senegal to Ethiopia, where it is found in dry, bush country. The female is like the male but lacks the crimson band on the throat. The total length is 12—13 cm (5 in). The nest is built of grass in dense bushes and sometimes also in a tree hollow or even an abandoned weaver's nest. It is a globular construction with the entrance hole at the side. The hen lays four to seven white eggs and the young hatch in twelve to fourteen days. The diet in the wild consists of seeds and partly also of insects.

In captivity, it is a hardy bird and easy to care for. A pair may be kept in a cage or in an aviary together with other birds. It breeds in confinement and should therefore be provided with a small, wooden nesting box which the male lines with nesting material, usually fine hay. The hen incubates during the day with the male taking over in the evening and both of them sitting on the eggs at night. If a pair is kept in an aviary with thick bushes they will build a nest of their own as in the wild. Sometimes the parents suddenly stop feeding the young for unknown reasons and such orphans may be given to a Bengalese Finch to rear.

The diet consists of millet, canary seed, hemp, rape, hulled oats and sprays of grass. Seeds of thistles and the like may also be given. Green food should be a regular part of the diet, and when rearing their young, it should also include egg mixture with supplements of Lucerne meal. A bit of curd is welcome and live insects should not be forgotten.

DIAMOND SPARROW

(Zonaeginthus guttatus) Estrildidae

This bird is one of the handsomest of small Australian birds. It measures 12 cm (5 in) in length and the sexes are alike in plumage, the male being recognized by his song. It inhabits grassy areas and bush country and is sometimes also found in parks and gardens on city outskirts. The domed, sparrow-like nest is built of grass in a thick bush. Sometimes, like the Silverbill, it erects the construction in the sticks forming the base of an eagle's nest. The clutch consists of four to seven white eggs and the incubation period is twelve to fourteen days. The Diamond Sparrow spends much of its time on the ground, where it eats various seeds.

Captive birds may be kept one pair to a cage or in an aviary with other smaller birds as companions. It is a hardy species, but does not stand up well to the rigours of travel from its distant home. Before embarking on such a journey the birds must be in excellent health. However, even so, they generally arrive in a very weakened condition and in poor feather, and require painstaking care before they are back in shape again. The Diamond Sparrow breeds in captivity, often in a wooden, semi-nesting box which it lines with various materials such as grass, hay, plant fibres, hairs, feathers, etc. Lengthy fibres are generally brought to the nest by the male.

The diet consists of small seeds such as millet and canary, green foods, e.g. spinach and chickweed as well as flowering grasses, a piece of apple and, when rearing the young, a 'Nightingale' egg mixture plus various insects and larvae.

INDEX OF COMMON NAMES

INDEX OF LATIN NAMES